Frederick the Great and The Seven Years War Life Stories for Young People

Ferdinand Schrader

Alpha Editions

This edition published in 2022

ISBN : 9789356310117

Design and Setting By
Alpha Editions
www.alphaedis.com
Email - info@alphaedis.com

As per information held with us this book is in Public Domain.
This book is a reproduction of an important historical work. Alpha Editions uses the best technology to reproduce historical work in the same manner it was first published to preserve its original nature. Any marks or number seen are left intentionally to preserve its true form.

Contents

Translator's Preface .... - 1 -
Chapter I The First Battle of the War .... - 3 -
Chapter II The Battle of Prague .... - 5 -
Chapter III Fredrick's Defeat and Seydlitz's Surprise .... - 8 -
Chapter IV The Brilliant Victory at Rossbach .... - 13 -
Chapter V Frederick at Leuthen and Lissa .... - 15 -
Chapter VI The Siege of Olmütz .... - 20 -
Chapter VII Seydlitz Saves the Day at Zorndorf .... - 26 -
Chapter VIII Frederick's Defeat at Hochkirch .... - 30 -
Chapter IX The most dreadful Day in Frederick's Life .... - 35 -
Chapter X The Battle of Liegnitz .... - 42 -
Chapter XI The Victory of Torgau Surprises Frederick .... - 46 -
Chapter XII The Camp at Bunzelwilz .... - 55 -
Chapter XIII The Dawn of Peace .... - 61 -
Chapter XIV End of the Seven Years' War .... - 65 -
Appendix .... - 69 -
Footnotes .... - 71 -

Translator's Preface

This little volume deals only with seven years in the life of Frederick the Great, but they were seven of the most memorable years in the history of Austria and Prussia—the period of the Seven Years' War, which confirmed to Frederick the possession of Silesia, and elevated Prussia to the first rank among European states. Three times Frederick waged war for its possession: the first time, in 1740-42, with Saxony, Bavaria, and France for allies against Austria and Great Britain; the second time, in 1744-45, when Austria was aided by Saxony; and the third time, in 1756-63, when Prussia, aided by some of the small German states and British subsidies, fought Austria, France, Russia, Sweden, and Saxony. The Seven Years' War was one of the greatest and most destructive wars of the eighteenth century, both to victors and vanquished. Frederick and his allies met with but five defeats in this war,—Kollin, Hastenbeck, Grossjägerndorf, Hochkirch, and Kunersdorf,—the last a most crushing defeat; but they won ten great victories, Lobositz, Prague, Rossbach, Leuthen, Zorndorf, Minden, Liegnitz, Torgau, Burkersdorf, and Freiberg; and in eight of these Frederick commanded in person, and in every case with a much smaller force than that of his enemies. Peace was finally made with Maria Theresa in 1763, and by a clear violation of ancient faith and treaty rights Silesia was taken from her. The various campaigns are described briefly and yet in such a manner that the interest of the narrative is kept up to the last, and the author, by the introduction of anecdotes, conversations, and fragments of letters, brings out very clearly the peculiar traits of the great king—his courage at one time, his despondent moods at others, his obstinacy and self-conceit, which more than once involved him in disaster, his humor and satire, his cruelty at times to his own troops, and again his fatherly relations to them. It is also a thrilling period of history with which the author deals, and replete with national as well as individual interest. Of the close of this great and sanguinary war, Macaulay says,—and he was not an admirer of Frederick,—"The proud and revengeful spirit of the Empress-Queen at length gave way; and in February, 1763, the peace of Hubertsburg put an end to the conflict which had during seven years devastated Germany. The king ceded nothing. The whole Continent in arms had proved unable to tear Silesia from that iron grasp.

The war was over. Frederick was safe. His glory was beyond the reach of envy. If he had not made conquests as vast as those of Alexander, of Cæsar, and of Napoleon,—if he had not, on field of battle, enjoyed the constant success of Marlborough and Wellington,—he had yet given an example unrivalled in history, of what capacity and resolution can effect against the greatest superiority of power and the utmost spite of fortune."

G. P. U.

CHICAGO, 1905

Chapter I
The First Battle of the War

What a glorious period of peace Germany enjoyed after the furious storms of war had devastated its flourishing provinces and brought ruin and death into so many homes! Prussia at this time had to stand the brunt of the storm, and had it not been for the indomitable spirit and great military skill of Frederick the Great, nothing could have saved the young kingdom from being forced back within the limits of its original territory. It was not the fault of its enemies that the effort failed. They left nothing undone to humiliate and subdue Prussia.

Maria Theresa was never reconciled to the loss of Silesia, which had been taken from her by Frederick in the preceding war with Austria. They said that she shed tears whenever she saw a Silesian. Cherishing such a strong attachment, it is not remarkable that the high-spirited Empress busied herself with schemes for the recovery of her lost province. With this purpose in view, she made secret treaties with Russia, France, and Sweden, and was also assured of the help of Saxony and many of the German imperial princes. Thus united, the plan was made to seize Prussia and reduce it to its old limits of the Mark of Brandenburg,[1] at the same time allotting Silesia to Austria, Westphalia to France, the bishopric of Magdeburg to Saxony, Pomerania to Sweden, and Prussia to Russia; but Frederick's sharp eyes discovered the designs of his enemies at an early stage in the game. Two traitors assisted him. Wenzel, a secretary in Dresden, and Weingarten, an *attaché* of the Austrian embassy in Berlin, were paid for warning him of the impending danger.

Frederick quietly and speedily formed his counterplans. He strengthened his army, concluded a subsidy agreement with England—which at that time was under the Hanoverian dynasty—and also secured promise of help from some of the German princes, particularly the dukes of Brunswick and Gotha and the Elector of Hesse-Cassel. With this comparatively small array he boldly prepared to oppose his powerful enemies. His motto was "Nothing venture, nothing have." He quietly placed his army upon a war footing, concentrated it at a given point, and then gave the order to march into Saxony.[2]

Frederick's army invaded that beautiful and fruitful country in three divisions, while Field-Marshal Schwerin, with a fourth, occupied Bohemia. In a few days its most important cities were in his possession. The invasion was effected with such startling quickness that the Elector and his family barely escaped being taken prisoners, but they were all treated with proper respect. The unexpected occupation caused great alarm all over Saxony, and the news of it created consternation at the Austrian court. Frederick was charged with bad faith and disturbance of the country's peace. The Emperor went so far as to characterize the bold intruders as outlaws. Frederick, however, was not disturbed. All that he cared for was the rupture of the alliance between the Elector and Austria. Not succeeding in this at the outset, he treated that province as an enemy.

The Saxon army, in the meantime, had camped at Pirna,[3] so as to be in easy communication with the Austrian forces, but Frederick shut them in so closely that they were soon in desperate straits. The Elector despatched messenger after messenger to Maria Theresa, praying for help. Alarmed at last by the bold operations of the King, she granted his requests and sent Field-Marshal Browne with seventy thousand men to the relief of Saxony, not doubting that he would crush Frederick at the first blow. Frederick, however, did not wait for the arrival of his enemy, but, dividing his force, boldly went out to meet him with about twenty-four thousand men, leaving the other half to watch the Saxons at Pirna.

The two armies met at Lobositz on the Elbe, October 1, 1756. The battle raged fiercely for six hours with little prospect of success for the Prussians, considering the superior strength of the enemy. Indeed, defeat at one time seemed inevitable, for their ammunition was exhausted. The brave Duke of Bevern, however, saved the army from its first defeat. When told that they were out of powder and shot, he coolly exclaimed: "Comrades, be of good courage. Charge with fixed bayonets!" His gallant troops obeyed, and hurled themselves upon the Austrians with such impetuosity that they were soon masters of the field. This was the first victory in the Seven Years' War. Frederick was delighted, and on that same day wrote to Field-Marshal Schwerin:

"I hardly need say anything to you about the troops. You know them. But never since I have had the honor to command them, cavalry as well as infantry, have they fought more bravely. It is easy to see by these brilliant achievements what they will do hereafter."

The news of the victory fell like a thunderbolt in the ranks of the Prussian King's enemies. The Saxon troops at Pirna, fourteen thousand strong, forced by bitter necessity and half starved, laid down their arms. The officers were released, after pledging themselves not to engage again in hostilities against Prussia. The common soldiers were placed at once in the Prussian army; but they were of no service, as they deserted at the earliest opportunity. The victory was followed by important results. It was the majestic prelude to the later battles of the Seven Years' War.

Chapter II
The Battle of Prague

Frederick improved the winter of 1756 by increasing the strength of his army and putting it in complete readiness for the field; for it was evident that the enemy, enraged at the glorious victory at Lobositz, would put forth its utmost efforts to crush him. Emperor Francis I,[4] upon the pretext that Frederick had broken the peace by the invasion of Saxony, induced the German imperial princes to place an army of sixty thousand men in the field, designated the Reichs Army. Frederick was confronted in all by half a million fighting men, while he could only muster the comparatively small force of about two hundred thousand. The disparity was great, and any other in his place would have been disheartened at once at the prospect before him, but Frederick did not waver or retreat. He relied upon his own indomitable spirit, the strong attachment and devotion of his officers, and above all upon his valiant, well-trained soldiers, every one of whom would have sacrificed his life for him. With such troops he could well afford to risk battle with an enemy greatly superior to him in numbers.

Without unnecessary waste of time, Frederick invaded Bohemia in the Spring of 1757. On the first night of the march, he decided to lodge with a peasant in a village near the frontier. Everything requisite was sent on in advance, and a royal servant notified the peasant that the King would sleep there that night. When the time came, the peasant went to his door to see the sovereign and his festive array. After waiting for some time he saw a man in a blue cloak, accompanied by two officers, dismount at his door. He asked this person whether he was one of the King's people; if so, he undoubtedly could be accommodated by his neighbors.

"I am not in the service of the King," was the reply of the man, who was none other than Frederick himself, "but he has invited me to supper with him."

"If that is the case, be so good as to come in, but brush off your boots, and clean up."

Various other generals and adjutants shortly drove up and saluted the King. The peasant, not knowing what to make of it, became alarmed and retreated into a corner. The King noticed his movement and said, "Stay here, sir, until the King arrives."

At last the peasant began to smile in a shame-faced way. "I know well enough who you are," he began. "You think I am a fool. This gentleman is the King himself."

Frederick smiled, and then entered the hut with some of his generals. The peasant thereupon came forward, shaking his head doubtfully, and when he had sufficiently regained composure, said to one of the attendants: "That is too simple a dress for the King of Prussia. Surely that gentleman could not oppress his peasants."

The next morning Frederick set off again in search of the enemy, who was in position on the heights around Prague. Before reaching that city, he had to march through the Pascopol pass. By way of precaution he sent one hundred and fifty hussars ahead to ascertain if the way was strongly guarded. Hearing a few shots, the hussars rode back to the King and reported that all the approaches to the city were securely defended by hussars and *pandours* (Hungarian soldiers). Frederick, who had already been informed to the contrary, sternly rebuked the commanding officer, and gave his own order, "Hussars! follow me. March!" They speedily brought in twenty *pandours* and seven hussars, who were found hiding in the bushes. The pass was difficult to travel, but it was unprotected, and on the same day the army got through safely and soon reached Prague, where the attack was to be made. The situation seemed favorable, as pasture land of unusual verdure appeared to stretch far in the distance; but Field-Marshal Schwerin advised the King to be cautious, for the meadow might be full of swamp-holes and bogs, in which cavalry and cannon might easily be mired. He also asked that his troops might have a short rest after their long and weary march; but, once having formed his plans, Frederick would listen to no suggestion of change.

"No, no," said he, "I must attack the enemy to-day, cost what it may. The fresher fish, the better fish."

The old Field-Marshal, notwithstanding his dismal forebodings, exclaimed: "Well, then, the battle must and shall be fought to-day. I will attack the Austrians here or wherever else I find them."

Frederick ordered the charge. Like the plunging billows of the sea the cavalry, with Schwerin at their head, hurled themselves upon the enemy; but the result was just what the veteran Field-Marshal had feared. Cannon and cavalry were hampered in their movements by the swampy ground, and while trying to extricate themselves were also exposed to a murderous fire from the enemy's batteries on the surrounding heights. Whole ranks of gallant Prussians were mowed down. It seemed impossible to fill the gaps, but at this juncture, Schwerin, then seventy-three years of age, seized a standard from a captain, and with the shout, "On, children, on, let those who are not cowards follow me!" rushed forward.[5] The brave old hero, however, had hardly gone ten paces when he fell, mangled by four grapeshots.

General Manteuffel took the standard from the hand of his dead friend and shouted, "Avenge the death of a great man! On, my children! Bravely on!" Nothing now could restrain the Prussians, who were furious with rage at the death of Schwerin. Notwithstanding the storm of fire which cruelly devastated their ranks, they heeded neither wounds nor death. They scaled the heights and deluged them with the enemy's blood. Frederick himself quickly ended the battle. He observed a gap in the enemy's centre, rushed in with three battalions, and held his position in the very thick of the fight. His soldiers fought like lions, and soon the victory was won. But at what a cost! Eighteen thousand brave Prussians were lying dead or wounded on the field, without counting the noble Schwerin, "who alone," as Frederick said, "was worth an army of ten thousand men." Such was the battle of Prague (May 6, 1757), one of the bloodiest struggles in the Seven Years' War.

Chapter III
Fredrick's Defeat and Seydlitz's Surprise

The Austrians fled into the city of Prague, which was closely invested by the Prussians and bombarded with red-hot shot. The people suffered greatly, and the prospect of approaching famine compelled them to make many sacrifices. The Austrian army had about given up everything for lost and was on the point of capitulating, when news reached them that Field-Marshal Daun, with a strong force of sixty-six thousand men, was on the way to their relief. Frederick marched out to meet him with thirty-two thousand men, the very flower of his army, hoping with this comparatively small force to check his advance. The two armies speedily met, and a battle began at Kollin. At the outset fortune favored the Prussians. The hussars cut their way through the enemy's lines so furiously that Daun was on the point of retreating. At this juncture, however, the King decided, in the very midst of the battle, to change his excellent original plan. Prince Moritz of Dessau and several other generals differed from him, and when at last he announced his decision, they refused to obey, for they foresaw it must lead to disaster. Drawing his sword for the first time, he rushed up to them, sternly reminded them of their duty, and ordered them back to their commands. The result was mismanagement and confusion in handling the troops. The Austrians and Saxons took advantage of this, and rushed into the gaps—for the Prussians were no longer in solid columns—and soon were the victors. The latter left fourteen thousand dead and wounded on the field. The remainder made an orderly retreat, and Daun did not venture to pursue them.

Bitterly disappointed, Frederick raised the siege of Prague and fell back with his shattered army to Nürnberg. They were obliged to dismount many times on the way to water the horses, and on one of these occasions an old trooper brought Frederick a refreshing draught of water in his steel cap, and handing it to him, said in the heartiest way, "Drink, Your Majesty, and let battles be battles. You are living—that is good. The Almighty also lives, and He will give us victory again."

The King looked at him and replied with a quiet smile: "Do you really think so, old fellow?"

The trooper nodded assent, and soon they were on the march again. The King was in an unusually gloomy mood, and at such times no one ventured to disturb him. When they reached Nürnberg he went off by himself without saying a word to anyone, and sat down upon an old waste-pipe, where he remained some time in deep thought, scratching curious figures in the sand with a stick. Observing this, his officers stepped more quietly and watched him with much curiosity. Suddenly he rose and said to those about him, "Gentlemen, it is time for action. We must not loiter."

Without showing any sign of his great disappointment over his defeat, he issued the necessary commands, and his aides were at once busy in distributing them. Even the appearance of his splendid guard, which had been so sorely treated at Kollin that out of a thousand men only two hundred were unharmed in the fight, did not disturb his composure in the least.

"Children," he said with much feeling, "you have had a hard day. But have patience, dear friends; I will make it all right yet."

The King's enemies were joyful over the news of his defeat at Kollin, and decided it would be wise to attack him on all sides. In the east the Russians invaded Prussia with one hundred thousand men. The Swedes, to prove their bravery, attacked Pomerania, but were driven back by General Belling. General Lehwald, however, was less fortunate in his operations against the Russians, as he had an army of only thirty-two thousand men. He was overpowered in an engagement at Grossjägerndorf and compelled to retreat. The Russians might easily have advanced to Brandenburg had they followed up their advantage, but their General Apraxin fell back still nearer the eastern Prussian frontier. This extraordinary movement can only be explained in one way. Apraxin had received express orders from the warlike Empress Elizabeth to press operations with vigor, but he had also been instructed by Grand Duke Peter to go slow and take matters easily, for he much preferred to have Frederick a good neighbor in the future than an enemy.

Thus the King's lucky star shone brightly when everything was darkest. He also received gratifying assurances of love and devotion from his own people. In Pomerania and Brandenburg they vied with each other in making good the losses of men and horses at Kollin. Frederick would have been delighted with these assurances had not fresh troubles overtaken him. His sorrow over the tragedy at Kollin was followed by bitter grief, occasioned by the death of a brother and his beloved mother.[6] His great sorrow, as well as his greatness of soul, is shown in his letters of that time, one of which closes with the words, "But I, threatened with the storm, and notwithstanding the approaching ruin, must act, live, and die as a King."

The French, meanwhile, who had crossed the Rhine and invaded Westphalia, one hundred thousand strong, were giving the King much trouble. His Anglo-German auxiliary army, led by the Duke of Cumberland, and much weaker than the French, had been utterly defeated by them at

Hastenbeck on the Weser.[7] The French now swarmed over Hesse, Hanover, Brunswick, and Westphalia, and destruction and ruin attended them wherever they appeared; for it had been decided in Paris to devastate Prussia and all the provinces which had remained faithful to the King. The French army, which at the beginning operated in two divisions, was now united with the imperial troops for the purpose of attacking Saxony, which was held by Frederick. The French afterward divided again, at Erfurt, into two bands, one of which under Prince Soubise levied contributions on Gotha and Weimar, while the other, under Marshal d'Estrées, levied still heavier contributions upon the city of Halle. From this point, one division of troops, led by the Duke of Ayer, pressed forward to Halberstadt and made inroads even as far as Magdeburg. Those were troublous times for the old mark.

Frederick, who was in upper Lusatia, was informed of the threatening operations of the enemy. He hastened forward by forced marches, strengthened his army by the corps of ten thousand men at Dresden under Prince Moritz, and with his comparatively small force advanced to the Saale by way of Grimma and Pegau. Bold General Seydlitz was in the advance with a thousand dragoons to clear the region of roving marauders. His brave troopers on September 7 appeared before Pegau, but found the gate on the farther side of the stone Elster bridge blocked and held by a large force of the enemy. Seydlitz had no infantry, but he ordered a hundred of his dragoons, for whom no horse was too wild, no ditch too wide, and who were splendidly trained, to dismount. They did so and stormed the gate, and then, carbines in hand, the troop drove the enemy at a gallop through the city. Seydlitz observed an Austrian hussar regiment in battle-order on the other side of the city. Although greatly outnumbered, without an instant's delay he dashed through their closed ranks with such fury that he captured three hundred and fifty of them and hotly pursued the others. The flying enemy attempted to make a stand on the bridge at Kösen and attack Seydlitz, but they were quickly dispersed.

Meanwhile Soubise and his French generals were occupying the castle at Gotha, and living there in luxurious style. His eight thousand troops were quartered in the market-place and other sections of the city and living upon the best of the land at the land's expense. Seydlitz, who was aware of this, decided to arrange a little surprise for them with the help of his merry troopers. Soubise and his generals were entertaining some foreign guests at an entertainment, for which extraordinary preparations had been made. The tables were loaded with the choicest viands, and costly wines flowed in streams. The guests were greatly enjoying the superb banquet, the charm of which was heightened by the presence of beautiful ladies, when suddenly Seydlitz and his hussars appeared at the gate. Everything was in confusion at once. The officers hurriedly left the festive scene, donned their gayly plumed hats, rushed out of the hall pell-mell, and fled in a panic. It never occurred to anyone, though they were eight thousand strong, to offer the slightest resistance to the little Prussian band.

Seydlitz, who could not think of making an effective pursuit with his few worn-out soldiers, contented himself with a short chase of the French. Covered with dust and sprinkled with foam after the sudden bold rush into the city, he and his officers laughed heartily at the deserted tables decked out so lavishly for the enemy. With lively jokes and many a rollicking troopers' song, the bold heroes refreshed themselves with the choice dishes and wines the duke's cooks had provided so lavishly, and passed the hours of the afternoon and night in the most hilarious and satisfied manner. An eyewitness says:

"Only a few French soldiers were taken prisoners, but an army of servants, lackeys, cooks, hairdressers, actors, and chambermaids, chests full of perfumes and pomades, powder-boxes and hair-nets, parasols and dressing-gowns, as well as a mass of those knick-knacks which are indispensable to French elegance, fell into the hands of the troopers, who examined their plunder with astonishment and fared royally upon the delicacies and wines found among the equipages and cooks' wagons, which Seydlitz turned over to his troopers. The other stuff he sent on to the French the next day free of charge, as Prussian troopers had no use for it."

Frederick, in the meantime, with his little army, about twenty-two thousand strong, had reached Erfurt, by way of Grimma and Naumburg, where he learned from Seydlitz that the fugitive enemy were occupying a strong position at Eisenach.[8] The situation was so uncertain that he decided not to venture far from Saxony and the Elbe. Believing that in his position he could resist the French advance, he sent Duke Ferdinand of Brunswick with four thousand men to Halberstadt to rid its people of the enemy's exactions, and Prince Moritz of Dessau with eight thousand men into the region between the Mulde and Elbe to watch the movements of the Austrians. When he heard of the departure of these forces Soubise's courage revived. He decided to advance and regain his former position. He also plucked up courage to place himself at the head of his army. With his strong force of eight thousand men he approached Gotha. As soon as Seydlitz, who had been reënforced by about fifteen thousand men, noticed this move of the enemy, he fell back, and pretended to seek shelter in a ravine. He ordered his troopers to dismount, fasten their sabres to their carbines, and spread themselves out in a long line near their horses. Thus extended, with the hussars in front and the dragoons dismounted and in position on the hillside, they presented from a distance the appearance of long lines of infantry. The French, believing the entire Prussian army was in front of them, fled precipitately. Seydlitz's troopers pursued them, and captured three officers and one hundred and fifty men. Truly the Prussians had no reason to fear such an enemy! As a result of the ruse, the French did not stop running until they were far away from Gotha.

About this time the Austrian general Haddick made a descent upon Berlin and levied a considerable war contribution, beside making a demand for twenty-four pairs of fine gloves, which he intended to present to his Empress. He obtained all that he demanded, including the gloves; but the Berliners showed a fine sense of humor in the trick they played upon him— for on his return home he learned that they were all for the left hand! Frederick, who received the news of the descent when it was too late to prevent it, decided at least to cut off Haddick's return, and advanced with four thousand men to the Elbe, leaving Field-Marshal Keith, with five thousand men, to guard the Saale. Other divisions were sent to Weissenfels and Merseburg. After the King's withdrawal from Thuringia, the French and the imperial troops also abandoned their position at Gotha, and advanced to Merseburg and Leipsic with the intention of occupying Saxony. Keith, in the meantime, however, had notified the King of the approach of the enemy, who, recognizing the danger, at once turned, drove the French before him, and made a halt between Weissenfels and Merseburg. This position, however, was insecure, for the greatly superior enemy was bent upon surrounding and capturing the King's little force. Indeed, Soubise carried his audacity so far that he sent word to his King that Frederick could no longer escape him and that he expected soon to have the honor of bringing him a prisoner to Paris. How bitterly he was deceived!

Chapter IV
The Brilliant Victory at Rossbach

Frederick encountered the enemy at Rossbach,[9] November 5, 1757. He could only oppose twenty-two thousand men to an army over sixty thousand strong. The disparity was great, but he relied upon his good fortune and the bravery of his soldiers. As was his invariable custom upon critical occasions, he sought to inspire his troops with words of encouragement.

"The hour has come," he said to them, "when all that is sacred to us depends upon our bravery. You know that I have shared fatigue, hunger, cold, night-watches, and dangers with you, and you know that I am ready to sacrifice my life with you and for you. All I ask in return is the same trust and good-will. Act now like men, and trust in God."

The King's simple words made a deep impression. His soldiers answered with an enthusiastic shout. "We will die with you!" exclaimed the grizzled warriors, while tears rolled down their powder-stained cheeks. The King was deeply moved by these expressions of love and devotion. He had chosen an elevated spot for his camp. The enemy was exultant, for they believed it an easy task to capture the little army, and they hastened to surround the site where it was camped so as to cut off escape in every direction. Frederick's sharp eyes watched their movements, but they did not appear to trouble him. On the other hand, he ordered his soldiers to eat their dinner, he and his generals at the same time sitting at open table. The French could not conceal their surprise at such recklessness. They were sure he was ignorant of his inevitable fate. They were not aware it was only a trick, for while part of the soldiers were eating, the others were getting the horses in order and artillery and ammunition in readiness. When all the preparations were made, and the King believed the right moment had come, the tents disappeared in a trice and the Prussians stood in marching order, ready for the attack. Before it began, the King noticed Möller, an artillery colonel, who was of great service to him in field operations, and who at all critical times, when his advice was asked, invariably said, "Believe me, Your Majesty, my guardian angel says it will be all right."

Möller had been assigned a very important position. The King had ordered his guns placed so that they were invisible to the enemy, and had hopes of good results from them. He hastened up to him, and placing his hand familiarly upon his shoulder, said, "Well, Möller, what does your guardian angel say this time? Is everything all right?"

"Oh, yes, Your Majesty," he replied. "My angel promises victory."

"At it, then, in God's name," answered Frederick, and at his signal the battle began. The artillery poured a terrible rain of shot into the French ranks, and the infantry accompanied the crashes of cannon with such a din of musketry that the French were taken completely by surprise. They had not recovered from it when General Seydlitz, hurling his pipe into the air and shouting "Forward!" gave the signal to his troopers to charge. Impetuously they dashed out from behind the hill, and hurled themselves upon the French like a thunderbolt, riding down and sabring everyone in their way. The panic-stricken enemy could offer no resistance. All who could, fled to escape destruction. The battle of Rossbach from that time on was simply a wild hunt. They threw away everything that might impede their flight. Cavalrymen dismounted, took off their great boots, and unbuckled their sabres. Whole battalions were taken prisoners by a few hussars without making any resistance, while others hid among the bushes or branches of trees. Few of them stopped until the Rhine was behind them. In short, it was a spectacle the like of which the world had rarely seen before. The attack began at two o'clock, and at nightfall not a Frenchman was to be seen. Two thousand of the enemy were left upon the field and seven thousand were captured Sixty-three cannon and twenty-three standards were also taken. The Prussians lost only ninety-one. All Germany was jubilant over the victory, for the French had made themselves bitterly hated by their outrages.

Immediately after the battle, the heroic King led his brave troops into Silesia, where the Austrians were once more active, having taken Breslau and Schweidnitz, and confident they would become masters of the whole province. In about a fortnight the Prussians reached the Oder. On the march thither, a fortunate event occurred. As the Austrians, four thousand strong, were taking the garrison of Schweidnitz to a place of imprisonment, the latter heard of the great victory their beloved King had won at Rossbach. Aroused by the news, they fell upon their guards and cut them down, and regained their freedom. Uncertain where they were going, they by chance met the King's army, of whose movements they were ignorant. Frederick, as delighted as he was surprised, cordially greeted them, and all considered the happy incident as a good omen for the future.

Chapter V
Frederick at Leuthen and Lissa

The main army of the Austrians, eighty thousand strong, held a position in the vicinity of Leuthen, between Breslau and Neumarkt. When its commander, Prince Carl of Lothringen, heard that the King was near by with thirty-six thousand men, he remarked, "That must be the Berlin guard parade." Frederick did not wait long. Regardless of the disparity between the two forces, he determined to measure strength with the Austrians, cost what it might. Under a gloomy, gray December sky, the King one day summoned his generals and thus addressed them:

"In violation of all the rules of the art of war, I propose to attack this army of Prince Carl though it is thrice as strong as ours. It is not a question of the numbers of the enemy nor of the strength of his position. I hope we shall overcome these odds by the valor of our troops, and by strictly carrying out my plans. I must risk this action or all will be lost. We must beat the enemy or all of us must perish before his batteries. So I think, so I shall act. Make my decision known to the army. Get it in readiness for the work soon to come. As for the rest, when you remember you are Prussians, you will certainly prove yourselves worthy of the name. But if there be any among you who fear to share danger with me, he can have his discharge this evening without exposing himself to the slightest reproach from me."

The King regarded his veterans questioningly. One of them came forward and said: "He is a knave who would retire or fear to offer his life for his Majesty."

"I was sure," resumed the King, "none of you would desert me. With your faithful aid, victory will be certain. Should I fall and thus be prevented from rewarding you for your service, the Fatherland will do it. Now go to your commands and give them this message: The regiment of cavalry which does not attack the enemy the instant it is ordered, shall be unhorsed after the battle and made a garrison regiment. The regiment of infantry which under any circumstances hesitates in the least, shall lose its colors and arms, and I will cut the decorations from the uniforms. Now, good-bye, gentlemen. We shall soon defeat the enemy or never see each other again."

Both officers and soldiers were deeply impressed by the King's words, and all awaited the battle of the following day with eager expectation. The soldiers were so enthusiastic that they sang sacred hymns to the accompaniment of the field bands.[10] As singing before battle had not previously been customary, one of the generals asked the King if he should not order the soldiers to be silent.

"No!" replied the King. "With such men as these, God certainly will give us the victory."

As the Prussians approached Leuthen, the King was informed that the enemy's force was as strong again as his own.

"I know it," answered the dauntless hero, "but there is only one way out of it—conquer or perish. I would attack them even were they on the Zobtenberg.[11]" Before giving the signal for the attack, Frederick called a hussar officer with fifty men to him and said: "I shall expose myself in battle to-day more than usual. You and your fifty men are to serve as my bodyguard. You must not leave me, and you must see to it that I do not fall into the hands of the canaille. If I am killed, cover my body with my cloak, place it in a wagon, and say not a word about it. Let the battle continue and the enemy will be beaten."

About this time the right wing of the cavalry, commanded by Prince Moritz of Dessau, halted at a churchyard, where the Austrians had planted one of their strongest batteries and were firing from time to time upon the skirmishers, sometimes with serious effect. To save them from this fire, Prince Moritz ordered them to fall back; but Frederick, when he noticed the movement, rushed up and cried: "Not yet! not yet! Those are only alarm shots. Children," turning to the skirmishers, "follow me."

They promptly obeyed the King, who led them back to their former position and said: "Stay here. Have no fear. I will send help to you."

While saying this, the enemy's cannonading was kept up. Prince Moritz said to the King: "It is too dangerous for you here, Your Majesty."

"That is true," replied Frederick, with the utmost composure, "but I shall soon drive the Austrians back."

The King made good his promise. The battle began between one and two o'clock, on the fifth of December, 1757. The enemy's line of battle stretched a mile, but Frederick was not alarmed. His main attack was directed against the left wing, and at this point the enemy's line was completely broken. A like fate overtook the right wing, which was simultaneously attacked. The enemy's centre finally gave way, and before dark the King was master of the field. The sanguinary struggle lasted only three hours, but it was one of the most brilliant of his victories. Twenty thousand prisoners fell into the hands of the Prussians, and beside these they captured one hundred and thirty-four cannon and fifty-nine standards. Frederick rewarded Prince Moritz on the field for his service. Drawing rein, he said to him, "I congratulate you upon the victory, Herr Field-Marshal"—with these words elevating him to that high position. The exhausted troops camped that night on the battlefield. It was a weird spectacle. All around them were the bodies left by the defeated Austrians, and the groans of the wounded made dreary night music. Suddenly an old grenadier loudly and jubilantly sang "Nun danket alle Gott."[12] This hymn of joy voiced the feelings of the soldiers, and when the bands struck up, the whole army joined in the uplifting song of thanksgiving. The effect was indescribable. The religious sentiment in the camp was unmistakable. Everyone had awaited the day with eager expectation. They had faced death in a thousand shapes, and terrible was the remembrance which it left. The pious soldiers passed a sleepless night, and left the field of victory with the proud consciousness that they had added new laurels to their heroic King's wreath of fame.

While in pursuit of the enemy, Frederick with a little band of soldiers approached Lissa. Before arriving he learned that it swarmed with Austrians. The King ordered a halt, reined up his horse, and sent one of his aides back with instructions to bring up the Manteuffel and Wedell battalions of grenadiers, which had been left behind at the last moment, and to say to them that he was so well satisfied with their bravery, they should spend the night with him at his headquarters in Lissa, and every man beside should have a thaler. It was a good half-hour before the two battalions came up, and when they did he placed himself at their head and boldly rode into Lissa, where everything was quiet, although lights were seen in the houses on all sides. As the King, who appeared familiar with the place, rode into the spacious plaza near the castle, and about sixty paces from the bridge across the Schweidnitz, he noticed white-coats coming out of several of the houses with straw on their backs. Most of them were caught by the Prussian grenadiers, and some were brought before the King. When asked what they were doing, one of them replied:

"A captain holds the other end of the bridge with one hundred and fifty men. He was ordered to strew the bridge with straw and set it afire as soon as the Prussians approached. So many townspeople have crossed, however, that the straw was trampled down in the mud and mire, and the captain threw it into the water and sent forty men to the stables to fetch fresh straw."

Some of the white-coats in the meantime had stolen away and notified the captain of the arrival of the Prussians, and while the King was talking with the prisoners he opened a brisk fire, by which some of the grenadiers in the rear of the King were wounded. Great confusion followed. The artillerists cried, "Back! back! we are fired upon!" Those on horseback rode near the houses, so as not to expose themselves to the fire of friend and enemy in the windows. The Prussian artillery opened fire at once, and the grenadiers also joined in. The entire city was in alarm. The Prussians were exposed to a brisk fire from the houses, to which they promptly replied. The tumult was great, and shouts and commands were confusedly mixed. The King, however, remarked with the utmost composure: "Gentlemen, follow me. I am no stranger here." Thereupon he rode to the left over the drawbridge leading to the castle, followed by a few of his officers. He had hardly arrived at the castle entrance when several Austrian officers and attendants, with lanterns in their hands, ran down the steps and made an effort to get to their horses in the castle yard and escape under cover of the darkness. The King, dismounting, quietly confronted them and said: "Good-evening, gentlemen. Evidently you were not expecting me. Is there no room left for me?"

It would have been easy for them to have overpowered Frederick if they had had the courage, but the suddenness of his appearance and the confident tone of his voice so completely dazed them that they took the lanterns from the hands of their attendants, lit the King up the stairs, and escorted him to one of the finest of the rooms. The most distinguished of the Austrian officers introduced his comrades to the King, by name and rank, and all joined in agreeable conversation. During this time more Prussian officers arrived at the castle, fearing the King might be in danger; but they found him enjoying himself mightily. He finally took leave of the Austrian officers, however, and they sought quarters in other rooms of the spacious castle.

"Good evening, gentlemen, evidently you were not expecting me"

That same night the King's entire army arrived at Lissa, having been ordered there by mistake. By this time the Prussians had taken a great number of prisoners. Zieten scoured the neighborhood with his hussars, and drove the fugitives even into Bohemia, and pressed the enemy so closely that out of eighty thousand men only about seventeen thousand reached the Bohemian frontier. The King followed, and soon overtook Zieten by a shorter route.

Chapter VI
The Siege of Olmütz

The year 1757, which had been so abundant in Prussian victories, drew to its close. Without remaining longer in Bohemia, the King made a forced march into Silesia,—where several cities and strongholds had again fallen into the enemy's hands,—not alone to drive the enemy out at that unfavorable season, but for the more important purpose of seeking winter quarters. As the Prussians were continually harassed on the march by the enemy's skirmishers, the King ordered night marches, so as to ensure the security of the sutlers' stores and baggage from the marauders. After marching all night, the army would halt at daybreak, the cavalry dismount, and the infantry sleep as much as possible under the circumstances. One morning the King, after dismounting, said: "How nice it would be if we had some schnapps!" Several, who had bread and brandy, rushed up to him and offered him their little store.

The King smiled with genuine satisfaction at the generosity and self-sacrificing spirit of his soldiers, and said: "Children, if I could drink brandy I would take it with pleasure. But I thank you for your love, and will not forget this day which has been such a happy one for us all." Then he turned to his staff, and said: "There is no happier King in the world than I." He ordered Lieutenant-Colonel Von Wacknitz to make a list of his guards, and at Breslau a *Friedrich d'or*[13] was given to each man. Notwithstanding these fatiguing marches, the King found his soldiers so eager for active duty that he decided to take advantage of their enthusiasm and attack the enemy without delay. Breslau, with its strong garrison of sixteen thousand men, surrendered, and this placed the King once more in possession of all Silesia except Schweidnitz. He now permitted his brave troops to go into winter quarters, as they so well deserved, while he spent the Winter in Breslau.

With the first approach of Spring the King was on the alert. When all was in readiness for moving, he mustered his guard on the Schweidnitz meadows. As they were assembling he noticed a seven-year-old lad who was actively engaged in drilling a dozen other boys, who had sticks for horses. The King laughed at the sport, and after watching them a little while, said: "That boy will be a good soldier some day." The next time he observed him, he saw that the little leader had exerted himself so vigorously in making an attack that he was bleeding profusely from the nose. The boy, however, mounted his stick again and renewed the attack with vigor. The King called to him: "My child, go home and wash off the blood."

The boy replied with much dignity: "Oh, no! that won't do, for it will throw everything into disorder. I am not yet killed; I am only wounded."

The King in surprise asked, "What is your name?"

"Kneuschke," replied the boy.

"So? And what does your father do?"

"He is a gardener."

The King made a note of it, and thenceforward paid the gardener five thalers a month, to be applied toward his son's education.

Satisfactory as everything appeared, Frederick was not unmindful of the dangers to which he was exposed. He would have been willing to make terms of peace if this had been satisfactory, but his haughty enemies did not stop to consider what serious losses their far abler adversary could inflict upon them, even with a smaller force. The more victories he won, the more implacable was their animosity toward him, and the more firmly convinced were they that sooner or later they would crush him; for they were sure that he could not hold out long against their united strength, and that in the end he would have to abandon the struggle from mere exhaustion. The King seems to have divined their schemes. About this time he wrote to a friend:

"What do you say to this alliance against the Margrave of Brandenburg? What would the great Elector have said if he had known that his grandson would have been fighting Russians, Austrians, nearly all Germany, and a hundred thousand Frenchmen? I do not know whether I am strong enough to withstand them and whether it would be a disgrace for me to submit, but I am certain that my enemies will gain no honor from my defeat."

After a careful survey of the situation, the King decided it would not be incompatible with honor to offer terms of peace to his enemies. They regarded the offer as a sign of weakness, rejected it, and entered upon a fresh campaign of even more active hostility.

Frederick did not hesitate. He rallied all his strength, repaired the losses incurred in previous battles, and confronted the powerful enemy with a splendidly equipped army. Unfortunate Saxony, which was completely in his hands, had to contribute a large sum of money, as well as clothing and recruits. Unexpected help also came from another quarter. The battle of Rossbach had aroused great enthusiasm in Europe, particularly in England, where there was strong sympathy with Prussia. Parliament unanimously voted to assist its brave ally. It sent him twelve thousand men, placed the Hanoverian army, which was in excellent condition, at his disposal, and united it with the forces from Hesse, Brunswick, and Gotha, making an army thirty thousand strong. This fresh body of troops, after such severe losses as he had met, was a welcome gift to the King. Parliament also promised to send four million thalers,[14] with the understanding that an able leader should be selected for the new corps. It could not have sent more acceptable help, for the King needed money as well as men at this time, when the war was about to be resumed with renewed vigor on all sides. Necessity forced him to make from ten to twelve millions of debased coin out of his four million thalers, as he had no other way of meeting his war expenses. He appointed Duke Ferdinand of Brunswick, who was universally regarded as a superior soldier, in command of the thirty thousand. Like the King, he, too, understood how to oppose a large army with a smaller one. Indeed, he was an expert in that direction. He drove the French, who had overrun West Germany, across the Rhine, inflicted heavy losses upon them in their retreat, and captured eleven thousand prisoners. Not satisfied with this achievement, he kept control of the river, and fought a battle with the French, June 23, at Crefeld, in which they were routed. Seven thousand more prisoners fell into his hands and hundreds of bodies covered the battlefield. Notwithstanding these disasters, the French a little later made another attempt to invade Germany, which was thwarted in such a masterly manner that at the close of the year they were content to stay on their own side of the German river. The Duke then made his headquarters in Munster and from there held the enemy in check.

While Duke Ferdinand was thus disposing of the French in the west, the King decided to attack the strong fortress at Schweidnitz, the only one remaining in the hands of the Austrians. On the march thither, while riding through a narrow defile, he found the artillery badly tangled up. While rushing about to hasten movements, he ran against a wheel and split one of his boots so badly that he could hardly keep it on. Impatient at the accident, he ordered an aide to find a shoemaker who could stitch up the boot. After considerable search a dragoon was found, who came, bringing his tools with him. The King, dismounting, and seating himself upon a hillock, said: "Can you mend my boot?"

"I will see, Your Majesty. I have mended a good many."

"Well, hurry up, so that I can go on."

The dragoon began work, at the same time growling to himself: "Hm! These boots have done service enough to warrant a new pair."

"What is that you are saying?"

"Nothing."

"But I want to know."

"Well, I think your boots have honestly done all the service they can. It is no wonder they rip. They are worn out."

"So? How long think you boots must last?"[15]

"*Must* last—that is a different thing; but I can easily tell you how long they *can* last—three years."

"Old fool, they are not as old as that yet. But tell me how a shoemaker can be a good dragoon."

"You might have seen how, at Hohenfriedsberg."

"Were you there?"

"To be sure I was, and I have soled Austrians so that many of them will remember me for a long time. When I make shoes, I am a shoemaker; and when I ride a horse, I am a dragoon—and Heaven help those who get into my hands!"

"Gently, gently, Mr. Shoemaker, I am in your hands. Be merciful with me." When the dragoon had finished, the King swiftly rode forward, placed himself at the head of his troops, and the march was resumed.

Frederick's fortunate victory so discouraged the Austrian troops that the Schweidnitz garrison, although amply provisioned, made but a feeble resistance, and surrendered in a few days at discretion. All Silesia was once more in possession of the King. To make Maria Theresa appreciate his strength he extended the area of his operations into Moravia and laid siege to the city of Olmütz, a suburb, as it were, of Vienna. It was an undertaking, however, as fruitless as it was unfortunate. The siege was long protracted, for the besiegers were not only hampered by lack of sufficient artillery, but of ammunition, which had to be hauled over morasses and through deep defiles. In consequence, the King had plenty of leisure for excursions into the neighboring country. Upon one of these occasions he rode about the country of Glatz in company with General Seydlitz. Passing through a defile, the King noticed, some distance away, a collection of people, whom at first glance he took to be a detachment of Austrians. Seydlitz, who had unusually sharp eyes, was of opinion that Fouquet had fixed his limits there and stationed these people so that the enemy's troops could not cross them without his knowledge. The King and Seydlitz rode up and found that the people were peasants of the country, whom Fouquet had placed there to watch the line.

"Are you Prussians?" asked Frederick.

"No," they replied, "we are Fickets." (Fouquet was called "Ficket" by the common people.)

"You can see now," said the King to Seydlitz, laughing, "who is master here, and that I don't count for much."

Notwithstanding this, the King continued riding about the country, and one day made a discovery which disturbed him not a little. He heard that the Countess Grün, wife of a staff officer of the garrison, had made a vow to the Virgin, at the Jesuit church, that she would present her a beautiful robe when the siege of Olmütz was raised. He immediately ordered a robe made of the richest material for the Madonna, and sent it to the Jesuits with the message that as he had heard of the Countess's useless vow, and as he was as mindful of the amenities of life as she, he did not wish our dear Lady should be the loser. As events might take another turn, he was simply carrying out what the Countess might not be able to perform. The Jesuits, delighted with his gift, came in procession to thank him, and exhibited the robe to strangers as a proof of the King's pious sentiments.

The King at this time evidently intended to press the siege with vigor and capture Olmütz. The Austrians by themselves would not have troubled him, but he soon heard the unwelcome news that the Russians had captured Cüstrin and committed frightful excesses. He was, therefore, forced to consider the raising of the siege. His final decision was hastened by the information that a detachment of the enemy had captured a convoy of ammunition and supplies at Domstädt, which had been sent him from Silesia. With extreme reluctance he summoned all his generals and regiment and battalion commanders to headquarters. When they were all there, he advanced into their midst and said:

"Gentlemen, the enemy has found an opportunity to destroy a convoy coming to us from Silesia. Owing to this fatal blow, I must raise the siege of Olmütz, but, gentlemen, you must not conclude that all is lost on that account. No, you may be sure that everything will be made good, and in such a way that the enemy will have something to think about. You must persuade your commands not to grumble about it. I hope you will not be disappointed yourselves, and should I,—though I do not expect it,—find that anyone else is, I shall punish such an one severely. I shall move immediately, and wherever I find the enemy I shall attack, however he may be posted and whether he has one or several batteries; but," tapping his brow with his stick, "I shall never do anything unreasonable or rash. I am confident that every one of my officers and soldiers will do their duty when the time comes, as they have always done in the past."

The King's words had a marked effect upon his generals. Frederick dismissed them with a cordial handshake and that gracious and friendly manner which captivated everyone. He parted from them with their assurance that he could rely upon their help under any circumstances. The siege was raised and the retreat was a masterly exhibition of generalship. It had to be made through Bohemia, as Field-Marshal Daun occupied the road through Silesia. Daun was taken by surprise. The hussars performed excellent service by covering the retreat through defiles and over mountains. The King rode at the head of the cavalry day and night, so as to be on the alert against surprise by the enemy. Swamps and hollows were not looked upon as obstacles. Artillery and cavalry were forced to find some way over them. Once, in the darkness of the night, the King, riding in front of the vanguard, came to a steep descent, some four or five hundred feet to the bottom. The skirmishers, with a Bohemian peasant who served as guide, were some distance in advance. For this reason the King, who was anxious to lose no time and to take advantage of the darkness, called a halt and notified the whole army of the situation. The cavalry had to dismount so as to reach the valley. One under officer who was in the lead hesitated on the edge of the descent, fearing that his horse would slip, and groped about himself for a footing while all the others were ready to go down. The King grew impatient over the waste of time.

"You must have even poorer eyes than I," he said with some anger, "for you stumble around like a blind man. Come here and hold fast to my coat-tails and I will get you down, and the army will not be delayed any longer." The officer did as he was bid and safely reached the bottom, like the others, with no greater harm than a few bruises.

Chapter VII
Seydlitz Saves the Day at Zorndorf

Notwithstanding obstacles of the kind related in the last chapter, which were frequent in that region, the progress of the army was not checked and Silesia was reached. The King left the larger part of the army at Landeshut with Field-Marshal Keith,[16] for the protection of Silesia, and pushed on by exhausting marches under the scorching sun to the relief of Count Dohna, who was in great danger from the attacks of the Russians. The latter, leaving devastation in their wake, had invaded Prussia as far as Cüstrin, as already mentioned. This place they had captured after great destruction, and they also forced it to pay a heavy contribution in money. Trampled fields and burning villages marked the route of the northern barbarians. The unfortunate inhabitants of cities and villages, driven from house and home, wandered in bands, seeking shelter and help. Deeply touched by the indescribable wretchedness of his countrymen, Frederick marched all the more rapidly until he came up with the Russians at Zorndorf. A little stream alone separated the two armies.

As so much depended upon securing an accurate idea of the whole situation, the exact position as well as numbers of the enemy, the King, attended by an aide, a servant who carried his spyglass, and a groom, rode to the bank of the stream, dismounted and bade his servant also alight. Resting his glass upon the latter's shoulder, he began making observations. The moment the Russians saw him, they opened a continuous fire from the nearest battery, the shot striking so near the King as to cover his coat with dirt. He calmly continued his observations without moving his glass or a change in the expression of his face. At last his aide thought it was his duty to remind him of the danger to which he was exposed. He stepped up, gently pulled the skirts of the King's coat, and said: "Your Majesty is in too great danger here. See how the shots are striking all around you. Your coat and hat are covered with dirt."

It was some little time before the King replied. At last he turned to the aide, saying with the utmost coolness: "If you are afraid, you can ride back"; and then resumed his observations at once. After he had seen all he wished, he said to his servant: "Now you can pack up." With these words he mounted his horse and leisurely rode away under a very shower of shot, talking in the meanwhile with his aide on various matters, utterly indifferent to danger.

The ruin caused by the Russians so infuriated the King that he decided upon a battle to the death, and issued orders that none of the barbarous enemy should be spared.

It was in the early morning of August 25, 1758, that the Prussian army, thirty-two thousand strong, confronted, in battle array, an enemy greatly exceeding it in strength, for the Russians numbered fifty-two thousand men. After all preparations for the battle had been made, and as the Prussians were marching out of camp, the King conversed with officers and the rank-and-file upon various matters as they passed by, with as much composure as if it were a parade. He was somewhat surprised at an old corporal in the grenadier battalion of the Berlin garrison, named Beek, whose very bald head was covered with the grenadier's cap while his wig was hanging from his knapsack. The King rode up to him and noticed that the old man was still very active.

"My friend," said he, "it is high time somebody looked after you. Have you had an education?"

"No, Your Majesty, I have learned nothing; I can neither read nor write. I had to be a soldier when I was very young, and I am of no use except to be shot at."

"How long have you been in the service?"

"Forty-four years already, and yet I am perfectly sound. If the war lasts long enough, however, my time to die will come. I don't care for that, for I have always lived the soldier's life. There is only one thing that troubles me. If it were not for that, Your Majesty, I shouldn't care if I were shot to-day. I would die right willingly."

The King listened attentively and then asked:

"Well, what troubles you?"

"Your Majesty, I have an only boy who is making some progress. His mother has taught him to read quite well, and I would be glad to have him learn whatever is proper for him, and go to some good school, so that he will know more than I do. That will help him when he goes out into the world, I cannot afford to give him anything out of my allowance."

"Where is your son to be found?"

The father gave him his son's residence, and told his name, and then the King rode away. A few minutes after this the battle began.

The Russians were formed in a huge quadrilateral. The Prussian artillery played havoc with this dense, unwieldy mass, for Captain Möller that day had one hundred and seventeen cannon and howitzers. Seydlitz was chief in command of all the cavalry. The Russian general, Fermor, opened the battle prematurely by a sudden attack with his cavalry, which dashed upon the Prussians with loud cheers. Seydlitz did not neglect his opportunity. With his characteristic energy he repulsed the cavalry and hurled back the enemy's infantry. The ensuing confusion, greatly increased by the dust, smoke, and furious battle cries, was so great that the Russian rear guard fired upon their own men. Dreadful slaughter followed, but the Russians stood as if rooted to the earth and fought like lions. At last, by the aid of invincible courage and judicious leadership, the Prussian army weakened the enemy, but as yet without decisive result. An eyewitness describes the further progress of the battle as follows:

"Fiercely blazed the noonday sun upon the exhausted troops, who had been on their feet since four o'clock in the morning. The cavalry was particularly fatigued, for it had been engaged at the most dangerous points. Both men and animals needed refreshment, which could only be procured for a short time back of the village of Zorndorf, where Seydlitz's squadrons had been stationed. The King was anxious to make the battle decisive, and therefore, in the afternoon, ordered it to be renewed. The Russian army stood ready in battle order. Fifteen thousand infantry, twelve ranks deep, occupied a strong position, and one hundred cannon covered their flanks and poured a deadly fire into the approaching Prussian regiments. Their onset was checked, and they fell back. The fate of Prussia and its heroic King hung in the balance. Seydlitz, who had formed his cavalry in three divisions, recognized the danger and rushed forward. He had his sixty-one squadrons in such shape that they could make repeated assaults upon the obstinate enemy. The first division was composed of eighteen squadrons of cuirassiers, assisted by a fine regiment of carbineers and a corps of *gens d'armes*. At a hundred yards away were three regiments of dragoons in the second division, which supported the first and filled up gaps. The third division, two hundred and fifty yards distant, consisted of three regiments of hussars, whose duty it was to capture artillery, take charge of prisoners, and destroy broken battalions.

"In order to save the badly weakened men and horses as much as possible, Seydlitz ordered that at first all movements should be made in slow and regular time; but at the final 'March, march,' they should not spare the spur, but hurl themselves upon the enemy with all possible force and fury. The powerful body began its slow movement, greatly hindered by the retreating battalions of Dohna's infantry. With clear, far-reaching voice Seydlitz ordered, 'Make ready for attack!' for the Russian shots were already falling among them. Quickly followed the first 'March, march,' order, blown by two hundred trumpeters, but the squadrons moved forward at an easy gallop. Nearer and nearer, enveloped in dense clouds of dust, they rushed upon the Russian colossus. Then came the thunder-shock. Grapeshot made frightful havoc in the Prussian ranks. At last the trumpeters sounded the final 'March, march,' and with all their force the Prussian centaurs hurled themselves upon the enemy's bayonets. With incessant and irresistible fury the whole sixty-one squadrons repeatedly charged. The cannon were captured, men were mowed down. Suddenly firing ceased. Death came by cut and thrust. Darkness and the complete exhaustion of men and horses ended the slaughter."

Frederick was jubilant over his brilliant victory. One hundred and three cannon, twenty-seven standards, and the money chests were the spoils of the day, but ten thousand Prussians were left upon the field of honor. On this day, Seydlitz and his cavalry had rescued the Fatherland and saved Prussia's military glory. He had performed miracles of bravery, and when the infantry wavered it was his cavalry which put the enemy to flight. The King himself acknowledged this, for when he was congratulated upon the great victory he turned to Seydlitz, and said: "But for this man things would have looked bad for us by this time."

Chapter VIII
Frederick's Defeat at Hochkirch

The King was in more cheerful humor after the brilliant victory at Zorndorf. The carrying out of his battle plans had demanded all his physical and mental ability, but he was not so absorbed in his victory that he forgot his old soldier. Shortly after the battle, he happened to meet Corporal Beek, who had escaped unhurt.

"Well," said the King to him with great cordiality, "your son is going to be looked after."

Beek soon learned that this was true. A messenger who carried the news of the victory to Berlin, when he returned, brought him a letter from his wife, telling him that her son had been taken from her by royal command and placed in the Gymnasium, where he was to be clothed, maintained, and educated at public expense. The old corporal wept tears of joy on receiving the news, and blessed the King who had such a fatherly interest in his soldiers.

A few days before the battle of Zorndorf a letter from the Austrian Field-Marshal Daun fell into the hands of the King.[17] It warned the Russian commander of the proposed attack, and added that he ought not to go into battle with such a wily enemy, but should cautiously manœuvre and hold him in check until the Austrians could get possession of Saxony. The letter disclosed the enemy's plans. After the victory, the King wrote to Daun:

"You did well to warn the Russian general against a wily enemy whom you know better than he. He made a stand and has been defeated."

A bolt from the clear sky could not have alarmed the Austrian field-marshal more than these words from the much-feared King, and his alarm increased when the rumor spread that he was approaching. The report was true. The energetic hero hurried forward as rapidly as the condition of his army would permit, so as to reach Saxony and bring relief to his brother, Prince Henry, who was hard-pressed by the Austrians. His plan was to drive the Austrians from Neisse, which had been besieged by them for a long time; but Daun, as soon as he was aware of Frederick's approach, withdrew in alarm and entrenched himself in a strong position. The King had no intention of attacking the enemy in his stronghold. He paid not the slightest attention to him, but as if in utter contempt took a position right before his eyes at Hochkirch, where on October 14, 1758, the battle occurred. The King evidently carried his audacious plan too far. He even allowed his enemy to go on entrenching himself without once disturbing him. The day before the sudden attack made by the Austrians he observed that they were throwing up defenses upon a mountain side, opposite one of the wings of his army, as boldly and openly as if they expected no interference. The Prussian general in command of that wing sent an aide to the King's headquarters with information of the enemy's operations. The King said to the aide:

"What good news bring you?"

The aide expressed his misgivings, and asked if his Majesty would order them to open fire on the enemy. The commander of the nearest battery had assured them the enemy was in range.

"No, no," replied the King, "pay no attention to them. I shall catch them in the morning."

He took his leave, but just as he was going out the King called him back.

"Listen! Have you any idea what a cannon-shot might cost me?"

The question surprised the aide, but he knew the King would prefer the best answer he could make than no reply at all, so he said:

"One shot might cost Your Majesty a *Friedrich d'or*."

"Well," continued the King, "and how many *Friedrich d'ors* do you suppose those fellows over there are worth?" At last the King said: "Well, you may fire a few shots, nothing more."

This was done, but the firing was useless.

Notwithstanding the insecure position of his army, the King had so little fear of attack that his generals felt it their duty to warn him and to try to dissuade him from his purpose. The camp was so poorly protected that Field-Marshal Keith one day said: "If the Austrians do not attack us here, they deserve to be hanged."

"Oh," replied the King, "let us hope they are more afraid of us than of the gallows."

The Austrian general's plans were so well made that the proud King had to expiate his contempt in defeat. On the 14th of October, before daybreak, Daun surrounded Hochkirch, in the vicinity of which the Prussians were encamped. They were resting in fancied security when they were suddenly roused by the dreadful thunder of cannon. The whole army was thrown into confusion. Soldiers ran over each other and could hardly find their weapons. In a wild scramble they tried to form in line, but no one could find his comrade, for the enemy's grapeshot was strewing the ground with bodies. The confusion knew no bounds; everyone was rushing about shouting and panic-stricken, the officers were powerless to check the tumult and disorder.

Zieten and Seydlitz, expecting the enemy's attack, had not allowed their men to leave their horses through the night. They endeavored to do something, but in the darkness they could not distinguish friend from foe, or escape the murderous fire which mowed down the Prussian ranks as if they had been rows of corn. Never did the sun rise upon a more dreadful spectacle. They turned their eyes away from it, and many of the grizzled warriors could not restrain their tears as they looked upon the awful sight. The signal for retreat was sounded, and notwithstanding the terror and confusion of the scene it was executed in such a masterly manner that Daun was astonished. He did not attempt to pursue, but fell back to his camp as if nothing had occurred. The Prussian loss was excessive. More than nine thousand bodies were lying in that narrow camp area. Beside this, they lost one hundred cannon and nearly all their tents and baggage.

The King had to summon up all his courage. At eleven o'clock that morning he had sadly gazed from an eminence at the fragments of his shattered army. He forced himself to assume a cheerful air, for he knew that all eyes were fixed upon him and that his soldiers were looking to him for consolation and fresh assurance. Therefore he appeared unmoved, and when General Von der Goltz joined him he said, in a facetious way: "My dear Goltz, they did not wake us up very politely."

"Excuse me, Your Majesty," replied the General, "we do not usually talk by day about the things which trouble us in sleep."

"You are right," said the King, "but some bright day I will return the incivility of these gentlemen who woke us up so rudely." Though only joking, the King had spoken prophetic words.

We know from the statements of those most intimate with him how deeply Frederick felt this matter. As, after the defeat at Kollin, his troubles were increased by the news of the death of his beloved mother, so now, in the very hour of his defeat at Hochkirch, he heard the sad news of the death of his sister Wilhelmina,[18] the sharer of his youthful troubles. But painful as this news was, when he reflected upon the dangers impending over the Fatherland he controlled his grief and devoted himself to his kingly duties.

Some days after this, October 17, the King summoned all his generals and staff officers and thus addressed them: "You are aware, gentlemen, that the army has suffered from a surprise. The darkness of the night was accountable for it. You must now consider our situation. We are in upper Lusatia. Our property, our wives, our children are far behind us. If we weaken in the least, all will be lost. An immediate battle is inevitable. Rather than submit, I will be buried with the rest of my army. I suppose that every one of you thinks as I do. He who does not, can be spared; he can go home immediately. Is there such a one among you?"

All present hastened to assure the King that they would do their duty as they had always done it. Frederick listened to their declaration with much satisfaction, and replied: "I am delighted, gentlemen, to find the same devotion and self-sacrifice you have always shown. I thank you for it."

His heavy losses at Hochkirch greatly troubled Frederick, but he consoled himself with the thought of his next great battle. At this time he wrote to a friend:

"The affair of October 14 ought to have decided the campaign, but it was nothing more than a scratch. A great battle must decide our fate. In all likelihood we shall have one very soon and then, with the result in our favor, we can rejoice. It has required many troops and much skill to get us thus far along."

While Frederick was occupied with his great plans to avenge his defeat, Daun remained quietly in his camp on the lookout, rejoicing over the disaster and confident that the Prussians had had enough of it. On the other hand, the King, who was always prompt in decision, sent speedy couriers to his brother Henry, in Saxony, with instructions for him to march into upper Lusatia with his seven thousand men and join his command. Meanwhile he kept a sharp watch upon the enemy. One Autumn morning, about daybreak, as he was riding out in search of information, attended by some under-officers, the fog grew so dense that they could only see a few paces ahead of them. They rode along a carriage road, the King having the idea that by turning to the right they could avoid the enemy's outposts. Adjutant von Oppen, however, noticed that they had already gone too far. "Upon my soul, Your Majesty," said he, "we are already too far to the left and are certainly behind the enemy's outposts." Scarcely had he said the last word, when an Austrian hussar appeared at their right to see who was talking. The King, with his usual presence of mind, advanced to the Austrian and coolly asked:

"Hussar, where does this road lead?"

The hussar saw at once they were Prussians, but he was so struck by the tone of voice and looks of the King, as well as by his coolness, that he stood as speechless and motionless as a statue. With the utmost composure, the King remarked: "Gentlemen, proceed. The hussar does not know." They rode quickly away under cover of the fog, which put an end to further observations. Frederick often related this incident afterward and laughed heartily over it.

Prince Henry soon arrived with his reënforcements. Thus strengthened, the King by skilful manœuvres succeeded in getting round the Austrians without their knowledge, and reaching Silesia, where the enemy was again trying to secure a foothold. Upon Frederick's appearance, however, the enemy retired. He believed he could drive the Austrians out of Neisse without serious effort and make himself master of Silesia. Daun was not a little surprised at the news. He was greatly astonished at the shrewdness of his adversary, and was much chagrined that the disaster at Hochkirch had not been of the least advantage to him. He longed to perform some great deed, and, as nothing better suggested itself to him, he decided to march into Saxony and wrest Dresden from the hands of the Prussians. But he reckoned without his host. Perhaps he believed that he could accomplish his purpose by merely demanding the surrender of the city. But he made a sad mistake. Schmettau, the commander, was not alarmed, and replied to the demand for surrender: "I will defend myself from street to street and finish up in the ruins of the Elector's palace." When Daun received this emphatic reply and was convinced that Schmettau meant what he said, he quickly withdrew, so that he should not be surprised by the King, and went into Winter quarters in Bohemia.

Chapter IX
The most dreadful Day in Frederick's Life

The year 1758 came to its close, and after a survey of his military operations it must be said that Frederick, notwithstanding many disasters, had made great headway against the legions of his enemies. He had again beaten them back and gloriously ended the year's campaign. His generals had also shown great skill in military operations. Belling, in particular, had bravely held his ground, and driven the Swedes back to Stralsund and the island of Rügen. Duke Ferdinand of Brunswick had been equally successful in his campaign against the French.

At the commencement of this year, war broke out first in Westphalia. The French attempted to overwhelm Duke Ferdinand by superior numbers. They despatched two strong armies against him, one of which went to Frankfurt and the other to Düsseldorf. The Duke decided to attack the army at Frankfurt, and fought a stubborn battle at Bergen. The French were in such strong position that the Prussians could not dislodge them, but were forced to fall back. The enemy pursued on foot and, harassed by superior numbers, they were forced to retreat to Bremen on the Weser. The enemies of Prussia held a jubilee. They were now certain that Westphalia, Hesse, Brunswick, and Hanover would be held by the French for all time, and that a sufficient force of commissioners would be sent over from Paris to establish French dominion over these fine German provinces. The Duke, however, did not entertain any such idea, for suddenly he again took the offensive and attacked the other army while on its way from Düsseldorf.

Ferdinand came upon the French camp at Minden and gave battle on the plains near that city, August 1, 1759. The attack began at the village of Todtenhausen. Count Wilhelm of Bückeburg, commanding the Prussian artillery, had taken a strong position. His fire played such havoc in the close ranks of the French that they were forced to fall back. The artillery was the first to retreat and the cavalry followed its example, which left great gaps in the ranks of the infantry and created much disorder. The Duke lost no time in following up his advantage. He ordered Sackville, the English general, to attack the enemy with his cavalry. There had been bad feeling between the two leaders for some time, so that concerted action between them was well-nigh impossible. As it was, the English general held back long enough to lose the advantage of the critical moment, so that the enemy, who could not have escaped annihilation had the attack been promptly made, had time enough to get into order and effect a retreat.[19] As it was, however, seven thousand prisoners were captured, and twenty-five cannon and several standards fell into the hands of the Prussians. The French were pursued for some distance, and did not find safety until they reached their camp at Frankfurt.

The news of this brilliant victory surprised the King just as he was in the midst of preparations for a terrible struggle with the enemy. He was in a strong position at Landeshut, and to the great astonishment of his enemies he remained there quietly until the middle of the year, apparently waiting to see what the Russians and Austrians were going to do. They had improved the intervening time in strengthening their depleted ranks, and now proposed to move against the Prussians in a body and with largely increased numbers. Frederick, all this time, was not unmindful of their plans, and considerably strengthened his own army; but even then he had only half as many troops as the enemy. The larger part of his choicest soldiers had been left on the field of honor, and it was with much anxiety that he regarded further campaigning. When news came of the Russian advance he was ignorant from what direction the attack would be made, as they were approaching the Brandenburg frontier in several divisions. To strengthen themselves and get in readiness for the great task awaiting them, it was decided that the brave Austrian General Laudon should unite his force of twenty thousand men with their force. Frederick, who was apprised of their plans, attempted to thwart them, and sent Generals Dohna and Wedell against them, but they were driven back, and the Austro-Russian combination was effected. The King had not believed this possible, and he was greatly surprised, therefore, by the news that the combined army, seventy thousand strong, was advancing to the Oder with designs upon the capital,[20] the road to which was open. The King now made his plans to frustrate the movement, and ordered the rapid advance of his army. He felt a fatal presentiment, and before he set out left his will with Prince Henry, and committed the administration of the kingdom to him in case anything happened to himself. He made all his arrangements with the same care that one displays when about to engage in a hazardous task. He provided for every emergency, and cautioned his brother against making a dishonorable peace after his death. With such gloomy thoughts as these the King advanced to meet his enemy.

On the eleventh of August, 1759, Frederick encountered his enemies fifty miles from Berlin. They were strongly entrenched at Kunersdorf[21] and surrounded by batteries of cannon, whose yawning mouths threatened death and destruction to anyone who came near them. Notwithstanding the great superiority of the enemies' numbers and the exceeding strength of their batteries, the King decided to attack the combined armies August 12. At that very time a courier from Duke Ferdinand of Brunswick arrived with the good news of the victory at Minden. The King now was in such confident mood that he ordered the courier to put off his return a few days, so that he could send back an equally joyful message of victory.

Toward noon the signal was given for attack, and the battle began with good fortune on the Prussian side. Encouraged by their King, the brave troops displayed again that heroic courage which had aroused universal admiration. They paid no attention to the awful fire which was devastating their ranks; with utter contempt for death they charged battery after battery, until the Russian left wing could no longer withstand their assaults. It was driven from its position and seventy cannon fell into their hands. It was a sign that the Goddess of Victory this time favored the Prussians.

By this time the day was nearly spent, and the soldiers, exhausted by their long struggle, aroused the sympathy of their leaders. Some of the oldest and most experienced of them urgently appealed to the King to stop the battle and spare the soldiers, as the enemy was retreating. Frederick, however, remained unmoved. He was not contented with the advantage he had gained. No, he would immediately annihilate the enemy. He ordered Seydlitz to cut his way through them with the cavalry. It was in vain, however, that Seydlitz explained he was holding Laudon in check on the right wing of the Russians. It was in vain that he assured the King the meadows before them were so swampy that horses and riders would be stuck in the bogs if they ventured there. All that he said was of no avail.

"Do your duty and execute the orders of your King," replied Frederick, firmly.

Seydlitz saluted and obeyed, but the soundness of his suggestions was realized only too soon. The ground shook under the squadrons as they got into motion, and soon they were floundering in the swamp. As if they were anticipating just such an inconsiderate movement, the Russians and Austrians furiously assaulted their immovable enemy, and such bloodshed ensued that the green meadows were crimsoned. Seydlitz himself was carried off the field wounded. The tired-out Prussians were panic-stricken. All fled who could, and the commands even of their highest officers were ineffective to stay the retreat. The Prussian army was not only defeated, it was destroyed. The battle was irretrievably lost, the ruin was complete. Pursued by the enemy, the unfortunates sought protection, and found it only in the darkness of the night.

The King had been conspicuous in his efforts to avert this disastrous defeat. He was in the very thick of the battle and did his utmost to keep the troops in line and encourage them. His attention was called to the danger he was in and he was besought to be more careful, but he emphatically refused, saying: "No! We must all strive for victory together, and I must do my duty like everyone else."

"Frederick stood on the bloody field like one dazed"

In the main attack two horses were shot down under him. Mounting a third, a bullet passed through his overcoat and shattered a gold case in his waistcoat pocket. All his efforts, however, were useless. His exhortations had lost their customary inspiring effect. Throwing away weapons and accoutrements, everyone sought safety in flight. He was not only compelled to witness the abandoning of the cannon captured from the Russians, but to mourn the loss of one hundred and sixty-five pieces of Prussian artillery. The situation became more and more desperate, and at last, realizing all was lost, he exclaimed in utter despair: "Is there not a cursed bullet for me today?"

When night came on, he was almost the only living soul on the wide battlefield. His army was partly scattered about the surrounding country; the rest of it had been put to flight.

Frederick stood on the bloody field like one dazed, and it was only by chance he was saved from capture by some Russians and Austrians who approached the spot where he was standing. Captain Prittiwitz, his fortunate star, happened to be passing near by, with forty hussars. Lieutenant Belten suddenly exclaimed: "Captain Prittiwitz, yonder stands the King."

The captain immediately turned his horse and rode forward with his men to the King, who was standing with folded arms upon a sandy hillock and alone, save for a single attendant who held his horse. His sword was sticking in the sand in front of him. The captain had considerable trouble in persuading the King to mount his horse, for at that instant Frederick was on the very verge of despair. To the appeal of the captain, he replied: "Leave me, Prittiwitz; I am lost."

"Not yet, Your Majesty," answered Prittiwitz; "you are still King of Prussia and commander of an army of brave soldiers."

"Well, if you think so, forward."

The hussars surrounded Frederick and made their way to the Oder, with roving bands of Cossacks continually swarming about them. Prittiwitz kept off the insolent pack and shot their leader off his horse. After the Muhl was safely crossed there was no further trouble, and the King was left uninjured at a ferryman's hut. He thanked the captain, ordered that gifts be distributed among the hussars, and gave instructions to see that he remained undisturbed until he had time to collect himself, for he was still overmastered by his calamity. He wrote to his minister, Finkenstein, in Berlin:

"Provide for the safety of the Queen and the royal family at Magdeburg, and do all you can for them."

A few hours later, he sent the following message to him:

"It is a terrible disaster. I shall not survive it. The consequences of the battle will be worse than the battle itself. I have no further resources and, to tell the truth, I consider everything lost. I shall not survive the destruction of the Fatherland. Adieu forever."

That was the most dreadful day in the life of the great King.

It is not surprising, however, that the King was in such a despondent mood, for on that very evening he could not have assembled five thousand men of his magnificent army. Twenty-six thousand were killed, wounded, or prisoners, and the others were scattered in flight. But the Russian army also suffered dreadfully. "If I should fight one more such battle," said its commanding general, "I should take the news of it to St. Petersburg myself with a staff in my hand." It was not long, however, before Frederick regained his composure. It was characteristic of him that he was always the greatest when things were going badly. Messengers flew to Berlin and Cüstrin with orders that artillery should be despatched to him as quickly as possible. He collected his fugitive troops, reënforced them with other detachments, and within a short time an army of eighteen thousand men was at his disposal. The most important thing for him now was to rouse the courage of his officers. To this end he sent for the messenger who had brought the news of the victory in Westphalia, and said to him in their hearing: "You have seen what has been going on here. Hurry back, and if you find the enemy is not in Berlin or Magdeburg, tell the Duke not much has yet been lost."

In view of Frederick's plight and the general condition of his affairs, this message must have seemed ridiculous, for he had not a sufficient force in readiness to stay the victorious advance of the Russians or to defend the capital and the country. This was known abroad also, for word was sent from Paris to the Russian general that the King of Prussia must be exterminated, and Berlin and the whole Mark of Brandenburg devastated. The Austrian Field-Marshal Daun also urged the Russians to make a rapid advance. Soltikow, their commander, however, did not move, and when further urged by Daun, almost suppliantly, to hurry forward, he simply wrote to him:

"I have won two battles, and am waiting before I advance again for news of a second one from you. It is not fair that my Emperor's army should have to do all the work."

Of course this jealousy among the enemy's leaders was of the greatest advantage to the King and the Fatherland. The Russians were in position at Frankfurt-on-the-Oder, and it was not until they were stirred up on all sides that they moved at all. When they did, they could not find subsistence, and at the end of October they went back again into Poland, which relieved the Prussians of one imminent danger.

Field-Marshal Daun in the meantime had been held in check in Saxony in a most masterly way by Prince Henry. The Prince was one of the ablest generals of his time, and his brother, the King, fully recognized it. He said of him once, "He is the only general who has not made a mistake during the entire war." Beside his strategic talent, he had engaging personal qualities which commended him to friend and foe alike. To him was assigned the duty of watching over the Electorate of Saxony. It may well be believed that he was an unwelcome visitor in the enemy's country, but he was greatly respected by the Saxons, and years after this they told with much emotion how this noble Hohenzollern in 1759, one day in harvest-time, when a sudden storm threatened to ruin their cornfields, allowed the peasants of a Saxon village to use his own horses for getting in their corn. He specially displayed his brilliant qualities in preventing Field-Marshal Daun from effecting a union with the Russians. By swift and skilful marches he kept Daun moving here and there, then suddenly eluded him, and destroyed a number of storehouses with supplies sufficient to have maintained fifty thousand soldiers for six months. This caused such a scarcity of subsistence and fodder that the indignant troops began to complain, and Daun had to fall back to a better position. The Mark of Brandenburg was safe, but other misfortunes were in store for Frederick. Dresden was in the hands of the enemy as one of the immediate results of the battle of Kunersdorf. When hardest pressed, Frederick wrote the commander in the Saxon capital to save if possible the seven millions of treasure in the money chests and evacuate with honor, for he could not send him help. This occurred immediately after the disastrous battle.

When Frederick was himself once more, he changed his mind, but alas! it was too late. Dresden was already lost to the Prussians. Frederick stamped with rage and declared he would retake it. He at once ordered the army to move into Saxony, although the inclement season of the year had begun. Prince Henry begged the King to spare his troops during the Winter and put off any large undertakings he had in view, but it was all in vain. The King would not listen to him. He ordered General Finck to attack the enemy's rear with fifteen thousand men and force him to retreat. Every tactician foresaw the disastrous consequences. All his generals were of opinion that the attack would end calamitously, and so it turned out. Finck had hardly reached Maxen, November 21, 1759, before the tables were turned. Instead of being the attacking party, he himself was attacked on all sides. Terrible slaughter ensued. The Prussians resisted the attack with their customary bravery, but finally had to succumb. The army was nearly wiped out, as eleven thousand of them were taken prisoners. Never before had a year been so disastrous for Frederick as was 1759. Never before did a year close more gloomily for him.

Chapter X
The Battle of Liegnitz

The deplorable result of these operations weighed heavily upon the King and never before did he inaugurate a campaign in a more despondent mood than that of 1760. It affected all his movements and all his actions and at last it seemed as if his lucky star would never shine again. In Silesia, the Austrian General Laudon, with a force three times greater, attacked General Fouqué, and his eight thousand men. Fouqué defended himself with the courage of a lion, and his soldiers fought none the less bravely, but he had the misfortune to be thrown from his horse in such a way that the animal fell upon him and undoubtedly would have crushed him to death but for the opportune arrival of his faithful groom. Only such troopers as had swift enough horses escaped from the scene of slaughter.

Frederick meanwhile was busy with his plans for retaking Dresden. He closely invested that city, but whatever moves he made were immediately thwarted by the Austrian general, who made a resolute defence of the post entrusted to him. The failure of his plans only made the King still more despondent. His best friends and most experienced generals suffered greatly from his ill humor, for he was often not only severe, but grossly unjust. He called the soldiers of one regiment cowards, and cut off the decorations from their uniforms beside taking away their sidearms and badges of honor. One blow after another struck the King. Hardly had he learned of the destruction of Fouqué's corps when the unhappy news came that General Laudon had taken the important fortress of Glatz. Everyone now expected another wrathful outbreak from the King, but on the contrary he remarked:

"Be it so! But they will have to give it back when peace is made. We must now go to Silesia lest we lose everything."

His decision was executed almost as soon as it was announced. While on the way, Daun was near him on one side and the Austrian General Lacy on the other. The three armies were so close together that they might easily have been mistaken for one. The light troops had frequent skirmishes, and hardly a day passed without encounters. Thus they fought their way along to Liegnitz. Further advance of the King was now impossible, for Laudon appeared in front of him. He was completely surrounded by the Austrian armies. The enemy's leaders were jubilant over the prospect of capturing the King and his entire army.

"The net is made in which we will capture the whole Prussian army," they said, contemptuously. "We have only to cast it."

The King was informed of their boast and laughingly replied: "That may be so, but I think I can make a hole in that net which they can't sew up again."

These were prophetic words.

The King's army now was so closely hemmed in by the Austrians that a mouse could not have slipped through, and the transportation of subsistence was impossible. Instead of commissary bread, zwiebach was distributed among the soldiers. The King often diverted himself toward evening by walking or riding among the squadrons of the *Garde du Corps* and talking with the men in a joking way, so as to keep them in good spirits and arouse hope for better times. Upon one such occasion he happened upon an under-officer who had broken his zwiebach and mixed it with a flask of red wine in the camp kettle, hanging over the fire.

"What kind of red soup is that you have there?" asked the King.

"Your Majesty," was the reply, "that soup cost me seven thalers in cash."

"Hoho! hoho!" said the King, "what is it?"

"It is red wine and zwiebach. I spent my last ducat[22] that I might have a little comfort once more."

"Well, if it has cost that much, I would like to know how it tastes."

"Certainly, Your Majesty, but I have only a tin spoon."

"That makes no difference."

Thereupon the King took a spoonful of the soup and said: "This is really very good, but it is too expensive. But I thank you just the same, and you must come soon and eat with me."

The King shortly afterward ordered the officer to come to his headquarters, and there he appesed his hunger with such food as Frederick ate. Beside this, the King gave him a handsome sum in gold. In such ways as these he managed to win the love and respect of his soldiers.

To the astonishment of all, Daun decided upon a battle, hoping thus to ensure the destruction of the Prussian army. The decisive blow was to be struck August 15, and to make it all the more decisive he arranged for an attack at daybreak and a repetition of the slaughter at Hochkirch. This time, however, Frederick was fortunate enough to hear of the plan and he made a counterplan at once. The Prussian army left its camp in absolute silence during the night and occupied the neighboring heights; and to make the Austrians believe it was resting quietly in its old position, peasants were employed to keep the campfires burning brightly.

Noiselessly Frederick arranged his army in fighting order. Silently the regiments stood in rank and listened for the signal to attack. There was something weird in the spectacle. The infantry stood with weapons ready for attack, and bright sabres flashed in the stout fists of the troopers ready at any instant to strike. Far down in the east day was dawning, and the silent host in the gray dusk looked like a troop of spectres.

To enjoy a moment's rest, Generals Seydlitz and Zieten threw themselves down by a campfire and slept; but Frederick, sitting upon a drumhead, considered the plans of the coming battle. At last he too was overcome by fatigue, and lying by the side of his generals was soon asleep. Suddenly a major rushed up and loudly asked, "Where is the King?"

The latter, somewhat startled, arose at once and answered, "What is the matter?"

"The enemy is not four hundred yards away," was his reply.

Frederick at the watch-fire before the battle of Liegnitz

Officers and men were at once on the alert. Two minutes sufficed to form the regiments in order. Words of command were heard on all sides. The cavalry made ready for the onset. The thunder of artillery resounded over hill and valley, and in less than ten minutes the battle was raging. Frederick's invincible spirit worked wonders. General Laudon had not expected such a reception and was utterly astonished to find a powerful force confronting him when he expected to surprise the Prussians in their camp. But in this emergency everything depended upon energy and courage. He made a brave assault, but the Prussians made a braver resistance. They fought like lions, and if it had been lighter the enemy would have been mercilessly slaughtered. When the sun rose it illuminated the field covered with bodies and broken weapons. The four hours' sanguinary conflict was decided. The Prussians won a complete victory, and the Austrians lost ten thousand men, beside twenty-three standards and eighty-two cannon. Thus ended the battle of Liegnitz, August 15, 1760.

Chapter XI
The Victory of Torgau Surprises Frederick

Cavalry and infantry were so exhausted by the bloody work that the King granted them a three hours' rest. Frederick went through the camp-lines, where there was great rejoicing over the victory, one of the most important results of which was the reawakening of the old battle spirit. There had not been such a glorious event since the disaster at Kunersdorf. He commended their valor, and assured them they should be rewarded at the proper time. The regiment which had lost its decorations at the close of the battle before Dresden behaved so bravely that the King uncovered his head before its commander and cordially thanked him. One old gray-bearded warrior, hoping that the King, while in this gracious mood, might restore to the regiment its trophies and sidearms, stepped forward and pleaded for them. The King quietly listened and then with much emotion replied:

"Yes, children, you have done handsomely. I thank you. You shall have everything back. All is forgotten and forgiven. But this day I shall never forget."

Loud cheers filled the air at the regiment's good fortune. After they were rested they formed on the field, strewn with the debris of battle, took the cannon and prisoners along, and made a three hours' march on that same day. This one victory placed Silesia, partly captured from the Austrians, in Prussian hands.

The King pursued the Austrians vigorously, and used his utmost endeavors to force them from their position. In one of his movements it became necessary to burn a village in the Silesian hills, to keep the Austrians from occupying a certain height. An officer, whose mother belonged in the village, happened to receive the order to burn it, and performed his duty without a moment's hesitation. This induced the King to interest himself in the family. He not only reimbursed her generously, but every time he met the officer he remembered the occurrence and inquired about his mother's health. The unconditional surrender of Silesia made that country very dear to him. He used to call it "The Pearl of his Crown," and used his utmost efforts to free it from the hated enemy.

Greatly to his disappointment, he was suddenly compelled to abandon further pursuit, for he learned that the Mark was in danger of falling into the enemy's hands. Forty-eight thousand Austrians and Russians had set out to capture Berlin, and reached the frontier unchecked. They knew that the weak city garrison was in no condition to resist the advance of such a strong army. The Prussian Residence actually fell into the hands of the Russian General Tottleben, October 4, 1760. Reports of cruelties practised by the Russians on the march had preceded their coming, and the people were greatly apprehensive of violence. Their apprehensions, however, were needless, as Tottleben was a very noble and humane man and exerted himself constantly to suppress all acts of violence. In reality, the Russians conducted themselves courteously as compared with the Saxons and Austrians, who committed outrageous acts of violence and vandalism.[23] For eight days they gave free rein to their rapacity and maltreatment, when suddenly the rumor spread and was publicly talked about that the King was approaching. Its effect was electrical. Taking all they could lay hands on, they hurriedly made off, for they feared his wrath. When Frederick heard that the mere rumor of his approach had so alarmed the enemy, he laughed loudly and said in the presence of his men: "And such louts as these would cope with us Prussians!"

He liked to joke with his soldiers, and took it in the best of humor when they joked back with him. On the march from Silesia to the Mark, which was a very quick one, the King often said to them when they were tired: "Straighten up, children, straighten up," meaning that they should march straighter and in better order.

"Fritz, we can't do it," was the reply; and one hussar, whom the King had personally addressed, said to him: "Fritz, I can't do it; I can't pull up my boots," at which the King laughed heartily.

It was on such intimate footing as this that the King stood with his men. He also knew just what demands he could make of them. They willingly made their utmost exertions on the long, hard marches. They would gladly die for him. He naturally shared all their troubles and deprivations. He had good reason therefore to write these words to one of his friends:

"You can have no conception of our dreadful fatigues. This movement is worse than any of its predecessors. Sometimes I do not know which way to turn. But I will not weary you with the recital of my troubles and anxieties. All my happiness is buried with the loved and revered ones to whom my heart clings. The close of my life is full of sorrow and pain."

As already said, Frederick found no enemy in Charlottenburg and its vicinity. Daun had fallen back to Saxony and taken a strong position at Torgau, so that by skilfully distributing his force he could drive back the Prussians and hold almost the whole country. Frederick found himself in a very bad position. The Russians were on the Oder in his rear, and in front the Austrians occupied an almost impregnable position. Under such circumstances it was difficult to find a safe way out. He hastily decided to move against the Austrians, but was at once deterred from so doing when he found their position was impregnable. It was now really a question of life or death. The King realized only too well that he could hardly have found a more disagreeable situation, but he did not disclose his anxiety. He forced himself to conceal his real feelings under a mask of cheerfulness rather than risk losing everything. It is even asserted indeed that in the last years of the Seven Years' War, when Frederick saw that the strength of his army was steadily diminishing while his enemies maintained their numbers, he carried opium with him with which to take his life if at last he had to succumb to their united strength. He said to a friend at this time:

"I shall never see the moment that forces me to make a disadvantageous peace. Either I will bury myself under the ruins of the Fatherland, or, should fate forbid me that consolation, I will put an end to my troubles when I no longer can bear them. I have acted according to the inner voice of conscience and honor, which guides and has always guided my steps, and my conduct will always be grounded on those principles. I sacrificed my youth to my father, my riper years to the Fatherland; now I think I have the right to dispose of my old age. I have said to you, and I repeat it, never will I put my hand to a disadvantageous peace. I am determined to finish this campaign and to venture the most desperate things, for I will conquer or honorably die."

How heavily his anxiety wore upon him at this time is shown in another letter to a friend, in which he says:

"I am slowly wasting away; I am like a living body gradually growing speechless, and losing limb by limb. Heaven help us! We need it. You always talk of me and my dangers. Do you not know it is not necessary for me to live? It is only necessary to do my duty and fight for the Fatherland and save it if possible."

In such a despondent mood as this was the King in the presence of the enemy at Torgau! What was to be done? If he quietly abandoned the place to the enemy, he must spend the Winter in his own country, already nearly exhausted. If he attacked and was defeated, he would lose all Prussia. He must venture everything, but before acting he decided to summon all his generals for a consultation. This took place on the morning of November 3, 1760. General Zieten, one of his most trusted friends, did not immediately appear, which greatly disturbed the King.

"Gentlemen," he said to them, "we can do nothing, for one of our number is not here."

He anxiously looked in the direction whence Zieten should come. At last the old general came riding up. Frederick hastened to meet him, embraced him, and said:

"Come, my dear Zieten, I have been anxiously waiting for you, for to-day will be a memorable one. Either I shall conquer or I shall end my troubles, for my position is very critical."

"What!" said the pious old Zieten, as he dismounted and stroked his beard, "do you doubt the help of God? He has stood by us often and will do so to-day. Your soldiers are full of courage. They trust their God."

These words restored the King's confidence. "Well, my dear Zieten," he replied, "if you think it all right, we will face the inevitable."

Taking Zieten's arm, they withdrew from the others for a time and had a confidential interview, after which he returned in better spirits. It was decided to attack, and the aides were soon flying in all directions, carrying the orders to the generals. The attack began that day.

The Prussian army was in two divisions, one led by the King, and the other by Zieten, who got in the rear of the enemy to attack his entrenchments. The King's division consisted of ten thousand grenadiers and was posted in some woods in battle order. When Frederick advanced with his vanguard upon Daun's entrenchments he was greeted by a murderous fire from two hundred cannon, so directed that even before the troops reached the enemy's lines they were almost unfitted for action, as they were deafened by the terrible crashes of the artillery. Notwithstanding the din and confusion, the King retained his composure, and turning to one of his generals, said: "What a horrible cannonading! Did you ever hear anything like it?"

The effect was frightful. In a short time nearly all the brave grenadiers were shot down. Their places were filled by fresh regiments and the cavalry was ordered to advance, but it was useless. Nothing could withstand that murderous fire. In the meantime Frederick himself was exposed to the greatest danger. Shots ploughed up the earth so near him that his horse was very restive. At last he had to make a show of composure. He rode from the first rank to the second, and came to a dragoon regiment.

"Well, children, how goes it? " he asked.

Some answered, "Badly, Your Majesty; we are standing here letting them shoot us down, and we cannot defend ourselves."

"Wait a little," said the King to them, "the firing will soon cease; then we will attack them."

While saying these words a cannon-ball came so close to him that his horse jumped to one side, knocked over a drum, and seemed about to run away with him. The King smiled, and said to the drummer:

"You tell the Austrians if they don't soon march off, I will take their guns away from them."

A new attack was ordered, but the Austrians resumed their destructive fire. At this crisis the King noticed there was a great gap on the right wing, between the *Garde du Corps* and the *gens d'armes*. He rode where the shots were falling thickest, to strengthen the weak spot. When this had been done, he remained there a short time, watching with his glass one of the batteries which was playing havoc with the *Garde du Corps*. A corporal of the fourth company remarked to a guard: "If we have got to stand here and be shot at, because they won't let us attack, give me a pinch of snuff."

The guard took his box from his pouch, and as he was lifting the cover, a cannon-ball shot off his head. In the most cold-blooded way, the corporal turned to his second neighbor and said: "Well, now, you give me a pinch; that one has gone to the d—l."

While Lieutenant von Byern, who afterward became leader of a cuirassier regiment, was speaking with the man about the accident, another ball killed his horse. The King, who had been watching them closely, rode up to the lieutenant, and then said to the corporal: "You have the proper coolness of a soldier. I shall remember you."

The corporal was overjoyed because the King had honored him by addressing him, which aroused his hope of promotion.

The *Garde du Corps* suffered greatly in this battle, for they were exposed to the fire of the battery already mentioned, and every discharge killed some of them. The King greatly deplored it, but he could not relieve them right away. He rode up to them and said in a tone of deep sympathy: "Children, only have patience for a few minutes. Things will quickly change."

At that instant a shot came close to the King and killed the file leader of the fourth company of the second squadron. His next neighbor said to the King: "Be careful of yourself, Your Majesty, and ride to a safer place. It is more important you should live than we."

The King turned a grateful look to the speaker and said: "My dear son, I thank you for your honest intentions and good-will. I shall not forget you."

Hardly had the King gone when a shot killed this honest man on the spot.

The attack was renewed by the Prussians, but their valor was of no avail against the strongly entrenched enemy. Night was approaching, but the Austrians had not been dislodged from their position. Firing was still kept up vigorously on both sides, and the combatants were shot down in rows. Frederick himself did not escape untouched. A bullet stunned him, and with the words, "I am killed," he fell. Two of his aides instantly ran up to him and searched for the wound, but his thick pelisse had saved him. Opening it, they found that the bullet had passed through his heavy clothing, but had not pierced his body. The King speedily came to himself and coolly said: "It is a matter of no consequence." The bullet, however, had made a bad contusion on his breast.

As night came on, confusion spread through the ranks, and Frederick was not a little disturbed about the result of the battle. He looked upon it as lost, and the Austrians were rejoicing over the victory they supposed they had gained. Both sides, however, were premature in their conclusions, for almost immediately the situation took on a new aspect.

In carrying out his orders, Zieten had had to contend with almost insuperable obstacles before he could get to the place to which he had been assigned. After almost superhuman exertions he reached, toward evening, the Süptitz heights. His soldiers dragged their cannon by hand and planted them on a hill near the enemy. With drums beating and cannon thundering, Zieten advanced to the attack, and at the very first onset captured a battery, causing great alarm and confusion among the Austrians. Field-Marshal Daun rallied all his forces and tried to drive the Prussians out of his entrenchments, but the effort was fruitless. Zieten, clearly realizing what was at stake, so continuously pressed his assaults that the Austrians could not withstand them. They began to waver, and General Daun was so badly wounded that he had to be carried from the field. This new misfortune increased their panic, and Zieten gave them no chance to get over it. He hurled his entire force upon them, and the victory was won.

The King, meanwhile, knew nothing of Zieten's successful attack and its important results, as the intervening darkness cut off his view of the field. Fancying the battle was lost, or at least that the victory was doubtful, he rode to the neighboring village of Elsnitz, where he went into a church, as all other places were filled with wounded. It was a very cold night. While tired-out, shivering soldiers sought rest and warmth by the watch-fires, Frederick sat upon the lowest step of the altar and by the dim light of a lamp wrote his orders for attack on the following day, for he was determined to make the battle decisive, whatever the cost. It was hardly daybreak when he mounted his horse and rode out of the village. He had not gone far when he saw a cavalry troop approaching, with Zieten at its head. In the tone of an officer reporting, he said to the King, "The enemy is beaten and has retreated."

Frederick was much excited by the announcement. With the activity of a boy, he jumped from his horse, Zieten following his example, and embraced his faithful general. Zieten cried like a child. Then the two rode back to the field, by different routes, to acquaint the troops with the joyful news and thank them for the bravery they had shown.

The King rode along the front, from the left to the right wing, and approached the generals who were gathered about the watch-fire. Frederick dismounted and joined the brave officers and men of his division, who were waiting for dawn to renew the attack upon the Austrians if they had not retreated. The King talked much with his soldiers and praised them for their valor. The grenadiers, knowing his amiability and condescension, crowded nearer and nearer about him. One of them, with whom the King had several times conversed and to whom he had often given money, was bold enough to ask him where he had been during the battle. They were accustomed to seeing him at their head, leading them into the thickest of the fight. This time, however, not an eye had seen him, and it was not right for him to forsake them. The King replied most graciously to the grenadier, saying that during most of the battle he had been at the left wing of the army and therefore could not be with his own men. While saying this, he unbuttoned his blue overcoat, as he was getting too warm. As he did so, the grenadier noticed a bullet falling from his clothes and saw the wound on his breast through the rent in his uniform. Excitedly he shouted: "Thou art still the old Fritz! Thou sharest every danger with us. For thee we would die gladly. Long live the King! Three times three!"

There was the greatest enthusiasm as Frederick rode up and down the line, shaking hands with this and that old graybeard and addressing a kindly word to everyone. On this occasion the old grenadiers were smoking wretched tobacco in their stub pipes right under his nose. An officer, who knew his dislike of tobacco, said to them, "Step back a little. His Majesty cannot endure tobacco smoke."

"No, children, stay where you are," replied the King, with a kindly smile. "I don't mind the smell."

He was thus gracious to his soldiers—for it was well known that he was averse to tobacco all his life—and in this and other ways was constantly manifesting his regard for them.

The loss of life at Torgau was very great on both sides. The Austrians lost twenty thousand men beside fifty-five cannon and twenty-seven standards, and the Prussians suffered almost as severely. Frederick, writing about it to a friend, said:

"We have just defeated the Austrians. They have lost an extraordinary number as well as we. This victory will perhaps allow us a little rest this Winter and that is about all. Next year we must begin anew. I have been hit by a shot, which grazed my breast, but it is only a bruise,—little pain, but no danger,—therefore I shall be as busy as ever."

Large as was the number killed in this battle, it was compensated for by its important results, for Prussia was saved and Saxony was once more freed from the Austrians. The Russians had retired again into Poland, and the Swedes had sought refuge in the farthest corners of Pomerania. The King decided to make his Winter quarters in Leipsic. On his way there, he reached a Saxon village near Wittenburg and took lodgings with a preacher. Delighted with the honor conferred upon him, he went to the door to meet the King, and said: "Come in, thou blessed of the Lord! Why dost thou stand outside?"

The King regarded the preacher, a venerable old man, with a kindly smile, and said to him: "How many taxpayers are there in this village?"

The preacher was so astonished at the question that he could hardly reply, although he knew the number very well. At last he collected his wits and said: "Twenty-two."

"And how much do they raise?"

The preacher stated the amount of grain in bushels as nearly as he could.

"Has the village suffered much during the war?"

"In the last eight weeks, Your Majesty, your troops and the Austrians have alternately foraged here. We are about at the end, for we only have our lives and cabins left."

"Who represented the Austrians here?"

"General Luzinsky."

"Where did he stop?"

"I had the honor of entertaining him in my house as well as I could."

"So? Did you also call him 'blessed of the Lord' when he came?"

"By no means, but I could not curse him."

"Oh, yes! You are a Saxon. Now I shall see whether I bring more blessings to this village than Luzinsky."

The King was shown to his room, and made much of the preacher, who greatly entertained him. When he departed he paid him a hundred *Friedrich d'ors*, and left an order that if Prussian troops came to the village they should take nothing, and should pay for everything they got outside their quarters.

Frederick always liked to talk with the country clergy. He resumed his march to Leipsic in more cheerful spirits, but did not enter the city at once. He had his night's lodgings at a parson's house in one of the villages near Leipsic. He was kept awake all night, for the house was overrun with mice, which made much noise in his room. Frederick arose at daybreak, called the pastor, and said: "Listen! Do you know anything about interpreting dreams?"

"Not particularly, Your Majesty, for I am not much of a believer in them."

"You may not believe in them, but many a dream has a real meaning. I will tell you of mine. I dreamed your rooms were full of mice. What does that signify?"

"I don't know."

"Well, I think Heaven means me to understand by this that my commissaries are good at plundering."

"Oh, no, Your Majesty, I fear your dream was the result of natural causes; for, alas! I am very much plagued by these vermin in my house and I do not know how to get rid of them."

"So? then I must be wrong. Now you take this *Friedrich d'or* and buy yourself a mouse-trap. Perhaps then I may sleep better the next time I come."

Frederick's enemies continued hoping that the time would come, in the execution of their plans, when they should find him exhausted by the weakness of his forces; and prospects indeed seemed to point that way. Doubtless he gained much by the victory at Torgau, but his situation still was a difficult one. He greatly deplored the losses his army had suffered, for he saw no way of replacing them. Signs of discontent were also beginning to appear among his troops because they were not regularly paid. This induced him, immediately after the battle at Torgau, to abandon his original plan of retaking Dresden. The following conversation shows how serious he was in this purpose. Immediately after the victory a grenadier asked: "Your Majesty, shall we now go into good Winter quarters?"

"We must first retake Dresden. After that, I will look out for you and you shall be satisfied."

In view of dissatisfactions among the soldiers and the approach of cold, rainy weather, the King decided, at the close of the year 1760, to go into Winter quarters.

Chapter XII
The Camp at Bunzelwilz

The next year began less fortunately than 1760 closed. The enemy determined to crush Frederick by weight of numbers. It was a long time, however, before military operations commenced. The King's forces had been so weakened that he dared not take the offensive without reserves to fall back upon. Nor did the enemy dare to attack singly. Every effort was made to overwhelm him by united strength. With this end in view, in August, seventy-two thousand Austrians under General Laudon joined the Russians, making a total of one hundred and thirty thousand men, while Frederick's army was hardly fifty thousand strong. Frederick had never before confronted so strong a combination.

At the beginning of Spring the King left Saxony for Silesia, most of which was in the enemy's possession. The march was made swiftly, for the Austrians were establishing strong positions here and there. One day, about noon, he approached a Saxon village near the Bohemian frontier, in the vicinity of which an entrenched position was held by a detachment under the command of an Austrian captain. As soon as he noticed the King's arrival at the village, he began a vigorous fire. Frederick was leaning against a shed, deep in thought, and at first seemed to pay no attention to the firing. His aides besought him to leave, as the place was too dangerous.

"The bullet which is to hit me," said the King, "will come from above."

A few minutes later a shot struck a post three yards away, quickly followed by a second. Remarking, "They are growing too discourteous," he ordered the destruction of the nest. The entrenchment was stormed and the captain and his men were made prisoners. The Prussian soldiers took his watch, purse, and whatever else of value he had about him, and at last cut off the gold ornaments on his hat. This he pronounced an insult, and demanded to be taken to the King. After a respectful greeting, the King said:

"Your servant, my dear Captain. What can I do for you?" The captain complained of his ill treatment.

"Do you not know the usages of war?" said the King. "This is not a processional. Thank God that you escaped with your life. My people are very considerate after all."

The captain was surprised at the light manner in which the King spoke, for, as he afterward said, he had always supposed the conqueror of Silesia to be a strong, imperious man.

The march was immediately resumed, and whenever Austrians showed themselves they were dispersed. Too weak to attack the Austrians at that time investing Schweidnitz, the King kept on to Bunzelwiltz, a very favorable position not far from Schweidnitz, where an entrenched camp was established in such a scientific and formidable manner that it looked like a fortress. The work of entrenching was rushed at every point, and officers joined hands with the soldiers in the work. Earthworks were also constructed in the churchyard in the village of Jauernick by soldiers sent for that purpose, who worked under the supervision of an officer. As they were throwing up the earth an old box was struck. They did not remove it with the usual care, but broke it open a little and found there was money in it. They would have instantly pounced upon it, but the officer drove them back and took the box himself, assuring them he would divide the money fairly when the work was done. They were satisfied with this, and the box was placed by the church door. The officer quietly retired to an unseen position, took off his stockings and went back with bare feet in his boots. He then took the box, shook the money out when unobserved, placed the stockings on the bottom of it and threw in what money it would hold. When the men were through with their work they asked for the box. The officer brought it at once, emptied out the money, and showed them there was nothing more in it but some old rags. There was great dissatisfaction, however, for they suspected the captain was not dealing fairly with them; seeing which, he threatened them with a stick. At this juncture the King came up to inspect the work. He asked what the matter was. They related the whole occurrence to him, whereupon he requested them to show him the box, the money, and the pretended old rags. An old grenadier, who had the latter in his hands, said: "Your Majesty, these are not old rags, but a pair of linen-thread stockings with a name on them."

Thereupon he showed them to the King, who clearly enough saw the name "V———" on them. The King summoned the officer and asked his name. He answered "V———."

"Well," said the King to the men, "don't you see the money belongs to him? His ancestors buried it here. Here is his name on the stockings, as plain as if it were put there recently. Stupids, what do you mean? Give the officer his money. I will have the box filled with genuine two-groschen pieces, and they shall be divided equally among you. Will that satisfy you?"

"Oh, yes, Your Majesty," was the answer of all. They were all the better satisfied as the coins in the box were mostly little old copper pieces. In this way the King saved the officer from the embarrassment naturally consequent upon discovery of dishonesty, and left him standing speechless and ashamed.

The defences were at last completed, and in that strong position Frederick awaited whatever might happen. As he was situated he could not undertake an attack, and was forced to act upon the defensive. Unusual precautions were taken in the camp. During the day the men slept by turns, and at night officers and men were awake and ready for action. As a rule the King left his tent every night, betook himself to a battery, and there awaited the morning under the open heavens. One night, as he was sitting upon the ground by the fire, enveloped in his cloak, he seemed to be tired and somewhat sleepy. A soldier of the Wolfersdorf regiment, noticing it, said to him: "I will make Your Majesty a pillow."

"How will you do it?" said the King.

The soldier took off his knapsack and fixed it so the King could rest his head upon it. He could not sleep, however, and so he talked with the soldier about his native land, his service, and other things. The latter asked the King several rather bold questions, which he answered very affably. The following conversation occurred between them:

SOLDIER. "If Your Majesty should be taken prisoner, how could you get released, as you are a King?"

KING. "As a general, not otherwise."

SOLDIER. "Hm! I don't believe that. You are more than a general."

KING. "No! With the army I am only a general."

SOLDIER (shaking his head). "They would get rich booty if they took you."

KING. "Oh, no, they would not. I have not a groschen in my pockets."

SOLDIER. "Your Majesty is trying to deceive me."

KING. "No! I tell you I have not a kreutzer" (and to convince him, the King emptied his pockets). "There! do you not see I am right?"

SOLDIER. "That is strange, but—you have a beautiful ring, which certainly is worth something."

KING. "Well—and what do you think it is worth? Give a guess." (Saying this, the King held up the ring for his examination.)

SOLDIER. "The ring may well have cost ten thousand thalers."

KING. "Fool! I will let you have it for five hundred thalers, and even then make money."

SOLDIER. "I would not believe that to all eternity. It is not true."

KING. "Certainly it is. Look here—I will count up the cost. This little stone here is perhaps worth three hundred and some odd thalers. The large one in the middle is a table diamond, which at the utmost did not cost over thirty thalers, and the rest of the ring, outside of the plain setting, is of no value."

SOLDIER. "I certainly wouldn't have believed it."

Day had dawned in the meantime. The King arose and ordered an aide, who had come up to make report, to give the soldier a *Friedrich d'or,* saying at the same time, "Are you convinced now that I have no money?"

Frederick often availed himself of the darkness to ride about and see what was going on. Once the King and Zieten, riding early in the morning, came to a little wood. Seeing no signs of an enemy Frederick began whistling softly, as was often his habit when not talking. All at once, as they ascended an eminence, Zieten noticed some of the enemy's troopers in the distance, wearing white cloaks.

"Be quiet, Your Majesty. Quick, put my white undercoat over your shoulders and ride slowly. They will think we are friends coming to meet them."

This evidently was the Austrians' opinion, for they seemed to be directing their course straight toward them; but suddenly the King and Zieten put spurs to their horses, changed their direction, and fortunately escaped. The King laughed and said: "My dear Zieten, that was a neat trick. Now, can I go on with my whistling?"

As was always his habit, the King continued to share all dangers and privations with his soldiers. Like them, he ate out of tin dishes and the hard ground was his bed whatever the weather might be.

"Take along a bundle of straw," he once said, as he started for a ride through the camp, "so that I won't have to lie on the bare ground, as I did last night."

The King was forced to remain inactive for three weeks in this distressing situation, for the combined Russian and Austrian forces were stretched out until they shut him in on all sides. He was in a critical condition. His stores were giving out and his troops were getting uneasy. He resolved therefore to risk a decisive stroke. It was fortunate for him that Laudon did not have supreme command, else he would have been crushed. The larger part of the army was under command of the Russian Field-Marshal Butterlin, who disliked Laudon and frequently quarrelled with him. This of course prevented coöperation. If one favored attacking, the other would refuse; if one gave an order to assault at a certain point, the other would issue an exactly contrary order. In this dissension lay the possibility of the King's escape, though he did not know it, for he had never heard even a hint of their enmity. His situation appeared to him desperate enough. Whichever way he turned he saw no prospect of escape. This greatly disturbed him. With an anxious heart he often hurried to old Zieten's little hut for consolation. This brave general confidently looked for better days in the future. His devotion and loyalty to the King never permitted him to doubt the success of his undertakings. In sheer desperation, the King would often say: "It cannot be done; it is impossible."

Whenever he said this, Zieten would reply: "Have courage, Your Majesty. Everything will come out right." Once he said this with so much assurance that the King quickly asked: "Have you secured the help of some new allies?"

"No," replied the general, "only our old help from above, which will never forsake us."

"Ah!" sighed the King, "the days of miracles are over."

"There is no need of miracles," replied the pious old hero. "He is on our side and will not let us be defeated."

Brave Zieten spoke truly, for three weeks afterward the Russians suddenly broke camp and departed. The cause was partly the disagreement between Butterlin and Laudon, but the principal reason for the sudden exit was the difficulty of procuring subsistence for man and beast. Silesia had been the scene of war so long and had been so ravaged that its people had to kill most of their animals for food and had been living for some time in a most wretched plight. It was manifestly impossible therefore to feed this great army. To save his, the Russian general had no alternative but to break camp and hurry off to Poland. How delighted was the King when he saw that he was freed from the enemy's investment! It was with a strange feeling he left the prison from which he had never expected to escape alive.

The close of the year, however, brought fresh trouble. The fortress of Schweidnitz, in Silesia, at last fell into the hands of the Austrians, and this strengthened the Russian force at Colberg, in the East. Frederick's immediate situation was not very enviable in any sense, for there had been a lack of subsistence for his troops for a long time, resulting in general discontent as well as disobedience. His financial resources were also well-nigh exhausted. But what made him most despondent was the great shrinkage of his numerical strength and the apparent impossibility of making it good. It was no longer possible to maintain discipline among his troops after they had been reduced to the bare necessities. The *Garde du Corps* and *gens d'armes*, who had been most loyally devoted to the King, now loudly asserted that if they were attacked, they would surrender. Such was the spiritless condition of his army! Is it any wonder the King was dejected as he contemplated the situation? Only his feeling of duty and his love for the Fatherland helped him to bear this heavy burden of trouble and care. In a letter written immediately after the taking of Schweidnitz, he says:

"This painful duty of service to the Fatherland is a heavy burden. With sadness I see its glory dimmed, its people despairing of deliverance, and devastation everywhere. Fatherland! Beloved name! Thy sorrows have moved me to devote the last remaining energies of my unfortunate life to thy rescue. Away with fruitless complaints—I will again take the field. Patriotism inspires me. A new day is dawning. I will revenge the State and end its troubles. I will forget my own distress and think only of it. My strong arm shall be its support. Notwithstanding his inclinations one must swim with the current, die for Fatherland, or accomplish his purposes."

Chapter XIII
The Dawn of Peace

The King entered upon another year with serious anxiety, for he could not escape the conviction that the longer the war continued the worse was his situation. His army was continually dwindling away. The old and tried troops, with which he had almost done wonders at the beginning of field operations, were now nearly all gone. His former sources of money had also run dry. Saxony, which until now had helped him greatly with its generous contributions, had paid out its last mark, and Prussia was so utterly exhausted that it could do nothing in any direction. With the enemy it was different. They confronted him with renewed strength and increased numbers. The combination of the two great armies was the most serious danger to his small force. It was by this combination that the fall of Schweidnitz was hastened. Frederick saw no prospect of victory anywhere, and yet the truth of his saying, "When necessity is greatest, help is nearest," was confirmed at that very time.

The Empress Elizabeth of Russia,[24] a faithful ally of Maria Theresa, died January 5, 1762. Both empresses, in alliance with France, had sworn to ruin the King of Prussia. Elizabeth's successor was Peter III, who was friendly to the King, and who at the very beginning of the war expressed his regret that Russia had taken part in hostilities against the King whom he greatly esteemed for his heroism. Frederick knew this, and hence was inclined to regard the death of the Empress as a fortunate event which would make for his success. He reckoned rightly, for hardly had Peter ascended the throne before he sent a messenger with orders to his army to retire from all of Frederick's provinces, to release all prisoners without further ceremony, and hand over the contents of the great storehouses in Pomerania to the people living there without cost. In place of a bitter enemy, the King had a warm friend in Russia. On May fifth, Peter made peace with Prussia; and not only this, but soon afterward he sent Czernichef with his twenty thousand men to join the Prussians. When this was known, Sweden, which had also been a party to the alliance, out of deference to Russia, decided to forego the pleasure of making war upon Prussia any longer. It did not waste any time in acquainting Frederick with its wishes. In fact, the proposition was made so suddenly that the great King facetiously said to the messenger who brought it:

"I was not aware I had been at war with Sweden. To be sure, I have heard of some dealings which my General Belling has had with that people, but they shall have peace if they wish it." The treaty of peace with Sweden was concluded May twenty-second.

How suddenly the aspect of his affairs changed! All at once Frederick was free from all danger, and was in a position to attack once more. Up to this time his weakness had forced him to act on the defensive. Now he was able to take the offensive, and make a stout resistance to his remaining enemies. He did not wait long, but marched his army with its Russian reënforcement into Silesia, to expel the Austrians and save that province from the enemy. Daun was seized with consternation when he heard of the King's advance. He hastily fell back, took a new position on the Burkersdorf hills, and entrenched himself as well as he could. It was Frederick's firm intention to attack the enemy at that point, and he had even fixed the day upon which he would measure strength with the foe, but an entirely unexpected as well as unfortunate event occurred, which frustrated all his plans and menaced both him and the Fatherland. After ruling six months, Peter was dethroned by conspirators, and died shortly afterward.[25] His wife, Catharine, was made regent by the dominant party. The shrewd Frederick may have anticipated such an occurrence, for, in all his letters to the young Emperor, he gave him much fatherly advice, and particularly entreated him to be prudent in his administration, and conciliatory in all his relations to his wife. This was a fortunate thing for the King, for when the ambitious Empress read this correspondence she was so deeply touched by Frederick's attitude toward her that she hastened negotiations for peace, declared she would have nothing to do with the war, and furthermore ordered her armies to return home at once.

The friendly sentiments of the Empress were very agreeable to Frederick, and yet he was greatly disappointed, as the Empress' order came just at the time he was about to strike a blow at the enemy. It was necessary to strike quickly, and yet he must act very cautiously. He knew the weak side of General Czernichef, his love of gold, and with this inducement he persuaded him to make a show of marching out with his army and occupying a threatening position, with the understanding that after three days he should return home. It was a rash act on the general's part, and one that might easily have cost him his head; but his good-will to the King, and his avarice, overcame all scruples. Frederick, happy that his wishes were now realized, vigorously attacked the enemy at Burkersdorf, while the Russians held their position, as agreed, a little distance off. Daun, who was ignorant of this arrangement, feared Czernichef and his strong force more than he did the King, and sent a considerable force against him. This was just what Frederick wished. This division of the enemy's strength made the battle easier, and the result was a complete victory for the Prussians. When the Austrians approached, the Russians retired, and on the day after the battle they began their homeward march.

Frederick now set out for Schweidnitz, and most skilfully and closely invested that fortress. His impatience at the slow progress of his laborers excited him to such a degree as to threaten serious physical consequences, and one day he decided to be bled in the open field. He inquired if there were a surgeon near by, and one was brought. The King alighted, took off his coat, seated himself, and the operation began. The cut was already bleeding, when a shell struck near the King, and sprinkled him and the surgeon with blood. The surgeon fled as fast as he could, leaving the King sitting. The latter was perfectly composed, and ordered him to come back and bandage the cut, adding some of his very emphatic threats. The surgeon finally returned in a very uneasy frame of mind. "I know your heart is in the right place; bandage the cut," said the King. Half scared to death, the surgeon did as he was ordered with trembling hands, after which the King mounted and rode away.

Notwithstanding all of Frederick's blustering the laborers made slow progress on account of the hardness of the soil, which the King did not take into consideration. He visited his displeasure principally upon his engineers. He spoke very harshly with a staff captain of that corps about the trenches, and at last in a burst of temper exclaimed: "Go to the d—l!"

The officer quietly withdrew, but the King called him back and said: "I wish that you would take charge of the work and then it may get on."

The officer at once replied: "Your Majesty, I am gratified that you will allow me to have a leg or an arm shot off before I leave the service, but I have great need of both, and beside, it will save Your Majesty the expense of carrying me back home."

The King was not displeased at his boldness, but laughed and ordered him back to work and handsomely remembered him.

The investment was now rapidly pushed on all sides and the fall of the fortress was inevitable. At this time Frederick had his headquarters at Peterswaldau, not far from Reichenbach, where he was much surprised by a sudden attack from the besieged. After the Austrians were driven back the Prussians strengthened their position, and the King decided that on the following day he would celebrate the victory by a general parade of the army. Frederick rode out from Peterswaldau with the Prussian princes to view the spectacle. A colonel from Schwerin, seeing him approach, rode quickly forward to receive his orders, but had the misfortune to be thrown from his horse, which stumbled. He was uninjured, and his horse waited quietly for him. The colonel remounted and galloped to meet the King as if nothing had happened. As they met, the King said: "You have had a fall!"

"Yes, but not from your favor."

"No," was the King's reply, "only out of the saddle into the sand."

The storming of Schweidnitz was successful and Frederick looked for important results to come from its fall, especially hoping it would revive the old battle spirit of his troops. This proved to be the case. Almost immediately came the glad tidings that Prince Henry, on the twenty-ninth of October, had completely routed the enemy in a sanguinary battle at Freiberg, Saxony. This was the last battle in the Seven Years' War, and good fortune did not again desert Frederick. As gloriously and successfully as he had maintained himself against the Austrians and Russians did Henry in the last year of the war maintain himself against the French, notwithstanding the meagre help he received. Though often forced to fall back, yet he always managed to advance again and successfully cope with the enemy. He so misled them by his extraordinary craftiness that his marches and counter-marches were a puzzle to the French. It was due to his military discipline and strategic skill that he won victories over a much stronger force at Billingshausen, Wilhelmsthal, and Luttenberg. Next he captured the capital at Cassel, November 1, 1762, and was preparing to take advantage of the favorable season to drive the French over the Rhine, when his plans were interrupted by an unlooked-for event. France asked for peace, and the King made no delay in seizing the opportunity to secure what he had long desired. The treaty between France, England, and Prussia was formally negotiated February 10, 1763.

Chapter XIV
End of the Seven Years' War

Maria Theresa and the Elector of Saxony realized that under such circumstances as these they were in no condition to continue the war alone against Prussia and that, whether they would or not, they must take steps to conclude a treaty of peace. The Seven Years' War had convinced both of them that they could never take beautiful Silesia from the hands of their brave enemies, much less humble the Margrave of Brandenburg. So they extended the hand of peace to the King. The hunting castle of Hubertsburg[26] was selected as the place for the negotiations and there the plenipotentiaries made peace, the King of Prussia being represented by Minister Von Herzberg. As he had fought many enemies in the field he had to make treaties with many, and they were concluded in such an honorable and skilful manner that Frederick was once more in possession of Silesia, and the county of Glatz did not lose a foot of its old possessions. The treaty was signed February 15, 1763, and caused unbounded enthusiasm in city and country. Those who have not experienced the horrors of war have little idea of the true significance of the word "peace." It recalls Schiller's beautiful words: "Gentle peace, sweet concord, abide with us. May that day never come when war's hordes shall devastate this quiet valley and when the evening sky, tinged with roseate hues, shall reflect the dreadful glare of burning villages and towns."

Crowned with victory, the King returned to his capital amid the rejoicings of his subjects. The Berliners had arranged an ovation for the homecoming hero. In view of the devastation and misery caused by the war he declined an immediate reception. On the thirtieth of March, a little later than he had intended, he entered his capital in the dusk of evening, remained there a short time, and then hastened on to Potsdam and Charlottenburg. At the latter place he one day summoned his musicians and fixed a time at which they should sing the chorale, "We praise thee, O God."

They assembled punctually, supposing that the church would be filled with a large and brilliant audience. Instead of this, the King alone appeared, seated himself, and gave them the signal. The singers began, and each one did his utmost to contribute to the success of the performance. As the music of the hymn of praise, majestic as a song of cherubim, filled the house of God, Frederick was so affected that he reverently fell upon his knees and with tears in his eyes expressed his sincere gratitude to the Almighty for his many deliverances and for the help which had been vouchsafed him through the long and dreadful war now so happily ended. It was thus the victorious King celebrated his peace festival, and his devout attitude was so impressive that there was not a dry eye among the singers. Never before had they taken part in such a solemn and inspiring ceremony.

Frederick always spoke freely of the battles in the long war and liked to hear the accounts of his generals. On one occasion General Seydlitz was dining with him at Potsdam. After a general conversation, mention was made of the battle of Rossbach, and the King said: "My dear Seydlitz, I am greatly indebted to you, to your officers, and to your whole division for that victory."

Seydlitz replied: "Excuse me, Your Majesty, not alone my division, but my chaplain, Balke, also conducted himself most gallantly. When the battle began he buckled on a sword and fought splendidly."

"You don't say so," said the King. "He must be rewarded in some special way for such unusual service. The Provost[27] has just died. Balke shall have the place." The chaplain was summoned to Potsdam, and was not a little surprised to receive an appointment to the vacant position.

The King extended his generosity not only in individual cases, but all over the country. There was urgent necessity to awaken fresh life and secure prosperity once more for the exhausted provinces. The war, which had been conducted with great bitterness and sometimes barbarity, had not only greatly distressed Prussia, but had left all Germany in a wretched plight. An entire circuit of towns and villages had been destroyed. The luxuriant fields had been trodden down by hoofs of horses and were lying waste. Entire villages were destitute of men, for their former residents had either been killed or driven away by the enemy. The Prussian army alone lost over two hundred thousand men during the war, and its allies, England, Hanover, Hesse, and others one hundred and sixty thousand more. The losses of the enemy were still greater, for they amounted to more than half a million men. Austria lost one hundred and forty thousand, Russia, one hundred and twenty thousand, France twenty-two thousand, Sweden, twenty-five thousand, and the German Reich, twenty-eight thousand.

Under such circumstances, it is not strange there were not enough men left in the country to till the soil. Women had to do that work, and in some places there were not women enough. Consequently the King issued an order to take a hundred of the strongest boys from the Potsdam Orphan Asylum, and set them at work in these depopulated localities. He devised still other means to make up this lack of men. He released Prussians from the army, filled their places with foreign recruits, and then ordered that as few Prussians as possible should be enlisted until the deficiency was made good. The number thus released was thirty thousand seven hundred and eighty. Every effort was made to assist them in the habits of self-reliance and industrial life, and orders were also issued that soldiers in such districts should be allowed to marry without a license from the authorities. Many buildings abandoned by their owners were going to ruin, and more than thirteen thousand houses in Prussia were destroyed. Fertile fields after the war looked like a barren wilderness, for there was a lack of seed-corn and products, and implements of every kind needed to put them in good condition again.

Gentry and peasants alike had been plundered by so many armies, and had lost so much by contributions and confiscations, that they were utterly destitute. The enemy had left them nothing but their lives. The country was not the only sufferer. Prosperity was ruined and trade was dead in the cities. There was no longer any regard for habits of order, and the police administration was wretched. The courts of justice and financial institutions had been reduced to inaction by these frequent invasions of the enemy. The silence of the laws had made the people reckless and produced in them an uncontrollable greed of gain. Nobles, merchants, farmers, and laborers raised the prices of their commodities, and their demands were exorbitant beyond belief. The situation called for drastic remedies, and the King, who was greatly concerned over the country's condition, did not hesitate to apply them in a practical way. He realized that the Provinces could not recover unaided, and so he decided to help them. By his orders Silesia had to contribute three million; Pomerania and Neumark, one million four hundred thousand; the Electorate, seven hundred thousand; the Duchy of Cleve, one hundred thousand, and the province of Prussia, eight hundred thousand thalers. Beside this, he distributed among the most needy localities twenty-five thousand bushels of rye and meal, and seventeen thousand bushels of oats taken from the public storehouses. He went even further than this. He reduced the army, and distributed thirty-five thousand horses among the peasants and gentry. In those parts of the country which had suffered most severely during the war, particularly Crossen, Hohenstein, and Halberstadt, the taxes were reduced one-half. In Silesia the payment of taxes was suspended for six months, and in Pomerania and Neumark for two years. The gentry also received considerable sums of money for the arrangement of their affairs and the payment of debts, for their resources had been so greatly impaired, money was so scarce, and credit so uncertain, that there was otherwise no hope for their recovery.[28]

It was not only cities and villages that were ruined during this war. The discipline of the army was so impaired by dissoluteness that more stringent regulations had to be adopted. The work, however, proceeded so slowly that permanent results were not apparent until 1775. From that time the army displayed the genuine military spirit. Everything except the regulations governing enlistments had been changed.

It was natural that by the reduction of the army many a deserving soldier found himself badly off. When the free battalions were organized, a blacksmith's journeyman in a Silesian village enlisted in the one commanded by Quintus Icilius, became a corporal, and subsequently was promoted to the position of major and was given the decoration for merit. After the battalion was disbanded, he was left to shift for himself, and as he could find nothing better went back to the smithy, but still wore his decoration. Seydlitz found him at work, and inquired where he got that decoration. He told his story, and Seydlitz told it to the King. Quintus was in attendance upon the King, and, one day at table, he said to him:

"Quintus, you had some fine specimens of officers in your battalion. There is, for instance, a blacksmith journeyman who has decorated himself with a service badge. How did that Cyclops come by it?"

Quintus replied: "I remember the brave fellow. I wish Your Majesty had had more such smiths in the campaign. This one certainly did well, and Your Majesty recognized his service and gave him the decoration in Saxony."

"Why have you not told me about him before?" said the King.

Quintus answered: "It has been done, but Your Majesty at the time was much prejudiced against the free battalions and struck the name of this brave fellow off the list."

The King smiled and shaking his head, said: "He has had hard luck and I must help him some way. Now, listen, I will give the man a pension for service, but he must not wear his decoration when at work and he must keep quiet until I call him."

The quondam major shortly after this received a kindly letter, which assured him a generous pension and made him the happiest of men.

Considering the care with which this sagacious sovereign looked after matters in general as well as individual affairs, and devoted himself to the humblest as well as the greatest in his dominions, it is not surprising that the ruined towns and villages, and the waste lands as well, soon presented a changed aspect, but it took years before the sorely oppressed country recovered entirely from the devastating effects of war. With the increasing industry of the people, however, and the unfailing encouragement and assistance of the King in advancing the interests of commerce, trade, and agriculture, Prussia in time rose to a higher degree of prosperity and culture than ever before.

Appendix

The following is a chronological statement of the principal events in the Seven Years' War:

1756 Frederick invades Saxony.

October 1, 1756 Frederick's first victory at Lobositz.

1757 Frederick invades Bohemia.

May 6, 1757 Frederick defeats the Austrians at Prague.

June 18, 1757 Frederick defeated by the Austrians at Kollin.

July 26, 1757 French victory at Hastenbeck.

August 30, 1757 Russian victory at Grossjägendorf.

November 5, 1757 Frederick's great victory at Rossbach.

December 5, 1757 Frederick defeats the Austrians at Leuthen.

August 25, 1758 Frederick defeats the Russians at Zorndorf.

October 14, 1758 Frederick defeated by Austrians at Hochkirch.

August 1, 1759 French defeated at Minden.

August 12, 1760 Frederick defeated at Kunersdorf.

August 15, 1760 Frederick defeats the Austrians at Liegnitz.

November 3, 1760 Frederick's great victory at Torgau.

January 5, 1762 Death of Czarina Elizabeth and accession of Peter III.

March 3, 1762 Peter makes peace with Frederick.

July 17, 1762 Peter assassinated and succeeded by Catharine.

July 21, 1762 Frederick's victory at Burkersdorf.

October 29, 1762 Victory of Prince Henry at Freiburg.

Last battle in the Seven Years' War.

February 10, 1763 Peace between France, England, and Prussia.

February 15, 1763 Peace of Hubertsburg and close of the war.

Footnotes

[1] The Mark or Margravate of Brandenburg was the beginning of the Kingdom of Prussia. The Nordmark, now in Saxony, was founded by Henry I in 928 to preserve certain German territory. In 1134 it was granted to Albert, who took the title of Margrave of Brandenburg. The mark was gradually extended during the next three centuries, and in 1618 the Duchy of Prussia was united to it. During the reign of Frederick William, the "Great Elector," it was largely developed, and in 1700 it became the Kingdom of Prussia.

[2] This was in the Autumn of 1756.

[3] Pirna is on the Elbe, twelve miles from Dresden. It suffered greatly not only during the Seven Years' but the Thirty Years' War.

[4] Francis I, son of Leopold, Duke of Lorraine, married Maria Theresa in 1736 and was elected Emperor of Austria in 1745.

[5] "Very certain it is, at sight of his own regiment in retreat, Feld-Marschall Schwerin seized the colors, as did other generals, who are not named, that day. Seizes the colors, fiery old man: *'Heran, meine kinder'* ('This way, my sons'), and rides ahead, along the straight dam again; his 'sons' all turning and with hot repentance following. 'On, my children, *heran!'* Five bits of grapeshot, deadly each of them, at once hit the old man; dead he sinks there on his flag: and will never fight more. *'Heran!'* storm the others with hot tears. Adjutant von Platen takes the flag; Platen too is instantly shot; but another takes it. *'Heran,* on!' in wild storm of rage and grief; in a word, they manage to do the work at Sterbohol, they and the rest."—*Carlyle's "Life of Frederick the Great,"* Book XVIII.

[6] July 5, 1757, Frederick wrote to his sister Wilhelmina at Baireuth: "We have no longer a mother. This loss puts the crown on my sorrows. I am obliged to act; and have not time to give free course to my tears. Judge, I pray you, of the situation of a feeling heart put to so cruel a trial. All losses in the world are capable of being remedied; but those which death causes are beyond the reach of hope."

[7] July 22, 1757.

[8] Eisenach is famous as the birthplace of Johann Sebastian Bach, the father of modern music. Luther also passed his early days there. Wartburg, the princely residence of the Grand Duke of Weimar, is there.

[9] A village in Saxony, nine miles southwest of Merseburg.

[10] Carlyle, in his "Frederick the Great," quotes the following verse from one of these hymns:

"Grant that with zeal and skill this day I do

What me to do behoves, what thou command'st me to;

Grant that I do it sharp, at point of moment fit,

And when I do it grant me good success in it."

[11] A famous solitary and massive eminence south of Leuthen, known as the "Magic Mountain."

[12]

"Nun danket alle Gott

Mit Herzen, Mund, und Händen,

Der grosse Dinge thut

An uns und allen Erden."

"Now thank God, one and all,

With heart, with voice, with hands,

Who wonders great hath done

To us and to all lands."

[13] About $3.50 in our money.

[14] About $3,350,000.

[15]"His wardrobe consisted of one fine gala dress, which lasted all his life; of two or three old coats fit for Monmouth Street, of yellow waistcoats soiled with snuff, and of huge boots embrowned by time."—*Macaulay's Essays*.

[16]George Keith was an English soldier, who fought for the house of Stuart in 1715, with his younger brother James. When that cause was lost, they went to the Continent and served under various flags, finally taking service with Frederick. Macaulay says: "Some of those who knew the palace best pronounced that the Lord Marischal (Keith) was the only human being whom Frederick ever really loved."

[17]This letter was written by Daun to the Russian General Fermor. The reply sent to Daun was written by the King, but was signed "Fermor," and read: "Your Excellency was in the right to warn me against a cunning enemy whom you know better than I. Here have I tried fighting him and got beaten.

"Your unfortunate "FERMOR."

[18]Princess Friederike Sophie Wilhelmina was the favorite sister of Frederick the Great. She was born in 1709, married the Margrave of Baireuth in 1731, and died in 1758. She wrote her memoirs, but they were not published until 1810. Like her brother, she was the frequent victim of her father's cruelty.

[19]Lord George Sackville, third son of the first Duke of Dorset, was an English soldier. He was made Major General in 1755 and Lieutenant General in 1757. He served second in command to Marlborough at Hanover in 1758, and upon the latter's death succeeded to the chief command. For his conduct at Minden he was dismissed from the army.

[20]Frankfurt.

[21]The battlefield of Kunersdorf is near Frankfurt, on the other side of the Oder, fifty miles southeast of Berlin.

[22]A ducat was the equivalent at that time of seven thalers.

[23]"In Charlottenburg, certain Saxon-Bruhl dragoons, who by their conduct, might have been the dragoons of Attila, smashed the furniture and the doors, cut the pictures, much maltreated the poor people, and what was reckoned still more tragical, overset the poor Polignac Collection of Antiques and Classicalities; not only knocking off noses and arms, but beating them small, lest reparation by cement should be possible, their officers, Pirna people, looking quietly on. A scandalous proceeding, thought everybody, friend or foe,—especially thought Frederick; whose indignation at the ruin of Charlottenburg came out in way of reprisal by and by."—*Carlyle's "Life of Frederick the Great."*

[24]Elizabeth Petrovna, born December 29, 1709, Empress of Russia from 1741 to 1762, was the daughter of Peter the Great and Catharine I. She was the founder of the Moscow University and St. Petersburg Academy of Fine Arts.

[25]Peter III was born in Holstein in 1728. He was the son of Charles Frederick, Duke of Holstein, and Anna, daughter of Peter the Great. He was assassinated, and his wife, who was an accomplice, succeeded him.

[26]This castle is near Wermadorf, Saxony, twenty-five miles east of Leipsic.

[27]An ecclesiastical officer.

> [28]The translator has taken the liberty to omit a few paragraphs in this connection, setting forth some of Frederick's financial and economical methods for the restoration of prosperity. They have only a local interest, and would hardly be entertaining for young people.

LIFE STORIES FOR YOUNG PEOPLE

Translated from the German by
GEORGE P. UPTON

8 Vols. Ready

BEETHOVEN

MOZART

BACH

MAID OF ORLEANS

WILLIAM TELL

THE LITTLE DAUPHIN

FREDERICK THE GREAT

MARIA THERESA

Each, with 4 Illustrations, 60 cents net

LIFE STORIES FOR YOUNG PEOPLE

*BIOGRAPHICAL ROMANCES
TRANSLATED FROM THE GERMAN BY
GEORGE P. UPTON*

A new, interesting, and very useful series that will be found especially suitable for school libraries and for supplementary reading

The books in this series are translated from the German, because in that country a specialty is made of really desirable reading for the young. Eight titles are now ready and more will follow.

Their simplicity and accuracy make them very useful for every school library in the grades.

For parents who feel disposed to give their children books that provide a mild element of historical information, as well as first-class entertainment, the little books will prove a veritable find.

The "life-stories" retain the story form throughout, and embody in each chapter a stirring event in the life of the hero or the action of the time. The dramatis personæ are actual characters, and the facts in the main are historically correct. They are therefore both entertaining and instructive, and present biography in its most attractive form for the young.

A FULL LIST OF THE TITLES IS GIVEN ON THE NEXT PAGE

The work of translation has been done by Mr. George P. Upton, whose "Memories" and Lives of Beethoven, Haydn, and Liszt, from the German of Max Mueller and Dr. Nohl, have been so successful.

Each is a small square 16mo in uniform binding, with four illustrations. Each 60 cents net.

FULL LIST OF TITLES
FREDERICK THE GREAT
THE MAID OF ORLEANS
THE LITTLE DAUPHIN
MARIA THERESA
WILLIAM TELL
MOZART
BEETHOVEN
JOHANN SEBASTIAN BACH

"These narratives have been well calculated for youthful minds past infancy, and Mr. Upton's version is easy and idiomatic."—*The Nation.*

"He is a delightful writer, clearness, strength, and sincerity marking everything to which he puts his hand. He has translated these little histories from the German in a way that the reader knows has conserved all the strength of the original."—*Chicago Evening Post.*

"They are written in simple, graphic style, handsomely illustrated, and will be read with delight by the young people for whose benefit they have been prepared."—*Chicago Tribune.*

"The work of translation seems to have been well done, and these little biographies are very well fitted for the use of young people.... The volumes are compact and neat, and are illustrated sufficiently but not too elaborately."—*Springfield Republican.*

"These books are most entertaining and vastly more wholesome than the story books with which the appetites of young readers are for the most part satisfied."—*Indianapolis Journal.*

Milton Keynes UK
Ingram Content Group UK Ltd.
UKHW040040180324
439604UK00006B/873